MY VIETNAM

Stories Of The War Years From The Inside Out

By Charlotte Stemple

CONTENTS   PAGE

PART TWO – DANANG

WHAT OTHERS SAY

Dr. Gary Benedict, President, The Christian and Missionary Alliance

Charlotte Stemple is a master story teller! As only she can, Char shares the challenges and victories of Alliance missionaries in war-torn Vietnam. Her stories reveal God's hand in her personal life and the lives of those around her. Through both good times and difficulties, Char and her husband, Woody, planted the seed of the Gospel throughout the country. You'll see this Asian country through the eyes of a young missionary, and you'll learn to love the people of Vietnam as God loves them. Thank you, Char, for a look into your heart and how God used you to impact a nation.

Ravi Zacharias, author and speaker

I have known Charlotte Stemple since the very early days of ministry when our paths crossed in a momentous period: during the war-torn years in Vietnam. In her book, Charlotte tells the story of Pham Hien, my interpreter who was imprisoned, as well as many other amazing adventures of people she and her husband met while serving in this beautiful but fragile country. Charlotte not only offers her readers rich cultural insight but also marvelous instances in which only God in his sovereignty could weave the threads of hope and healing.

Dr. Marvin L. Eyler, Former Chaplain, First Marine Division, Danang, South Vietnam 1970-71

Charlotte Stemple's exciting and informative new memoir about the daily life of a missionary couple bringing the good news of the Gospel to Vietnamese during the tense Vietnam war years is compelling reading. This book is enjoyable as it focuses on many personal encounters that Charlotte had while trying to assist the Vietnamese Church in the midst of the dangerous political and military conflict, and still be a wife and mother.

I recommend this captivating book to lay persons interested in mission outreach; to mission historians studying the expansion of the Church in southeast Asia; and to military veterans who also shared in the Vietnam experience.

Dr. Robert Fetherlin, Vice President, Overseas Ministries, The C&MA

Since The Christian and Missionary Alliance of North America began its investment in the people of Vietnam a century ago, the Tin Lanh family of Alliance churches there has grown to more than one and a half million members and adherents. But this has come at significant cost. As Dr. Charlotte Stemple expresses in these pages, some missionaries laid down their lives in Vietnam as a part of the huge investment that's been made. Dr. Stemple's wonderful story-telling ability enables the reader to journey with her and her husband, Woody, during their years of participating in what God has done through the Alliance in Vietnam. There are laughter and tears, worship and trials in these pages. I hope you'll enjoy reading them as much as I have.

Susan Bernard, National Director of Alliance Women Ministries, The C&MA

I found this a compelling, colorful collection of stories from the Vietnam war years which gives insight into the culture of the wonderful people who live in this land. It is told in an easy to read and often humorous way. The experiences will enrich your life.

Hallie Cirino, EdM, Harvard Graduate School of Education

As a lifelong educator who has worked with many high school students and teachers over the years, I find *My Vietnam* a refreshing counterpoint to most stories about the Vietnam War. The usual "boots on the ground" viewpoint is (and should be) gritty and horrific, but *My Vietnam* shows the other side to life during the war. Cultural nuances including food, religion, housing, language, poverty, and relationships are clearly and respectfully illuminated by Charlotte Stemple's sensitive and often humorous take on her experiences as a missionary, based in Vietnam during this unforgettable time in history. To provide the bigger and more complete picture, consider *My Vietnam* a must read for students who are studying this controversial war.

Beth and Rick Drummond – retired C&MA international workers in Vietnam, Indonesia, Cambodia. Locating and ministering to Vietnamese-at-risk in Cambodia since 1996

We haven't just heard about Char but have known and worked with her for over 40 years. She's the same outside the book as she is in the book. She is deeply spiritual, but real and human. She is genuine, sensitive, deeply loves the Lord and people of many cultures but especially the Vietnamese. As you read her stories you will laugh, cry and come away changed.

Mark W. Sasse, Chair, Social Studies Department, Dalat International School, Penang, Malaysia

From rubbing elbows with Bob Hope's USO tour, to lighting Ted Kennedy's cigar, to catching life-saving rides on military transports, to hunkering down in their home listening to the shelling around them, *My Vietnam* chronicles the fascinating lives of the Stemple family ministering to the Vietnamese people during the most turbulent years of the Vietnam War. Unlike the star-studded cast who made their cameo appearances, stated their political views and left, the Stemples and many other volunteers like them lived as the unsung heroes of the war – helping the crippled, educating the poor and communicating hope into many dark and dreary lives. *My Vietnam* is the remarkable story of one family and their faith and compassion which reached out to an untold number of lives during one of the modern era's most tragic periods. The Stemples' story is a testament to the power of faith and courage which should serve as a model for anyone daring to make a difference in this world.

Peter Burgo, Editor Alliance Life (alife) Magazine

Nothing seizes the heart like a great story told well. I have met few storytellers as poignant and compelling as Charlotte Stemple. Her accounts of her families' trials and triumphs as missionaries in Vietnam have made me laugh and cry; cheer and grieve; shout and fall silent—in awe of God's relentless pursuit of His lost ones. So be forewarned: unless you're willing to endure some serious eyestrain,

DON"T PICK UP THIS BOOK—because you won't want to put it back down.

Lois Olmstead, author, speaker, columnist

I just finishing reading *My Vietnam*. Tears are running down my face. This is not just a missionary book. This is an "inside the heart and soul of a missionary" book. Stemple's well written, easy to read style transports the reader from her home in Vietnam to the back of the bicycle tri-shaw to the prison camp where she used her nursing skills to show God's love in real life. I will treasure my copy of the book and share many with friends. I was afraid that the Charlotte Stemple I know, love and admire, would not come through in the printed page—I was wrong—she did!!!!

Tuyet Collacott, translator from Quang Ngai

Even though it was over forty years ago, Charlotte's stories are so lively in detail that I thought they had just happened recently. This book brings back so many both beautiful and sad memories so dear to me. What a wonderful treat to read this account of missionary life in Vietnam full of danger, death, joy and laughter. It will be a blessing to anyone who reads it. You made the Vietnamese culture come through so vividly but not ever in an offensive way; on the contrary, I always noted a great sense of humor between the lines when you explain the culture that was so foreign to you as an American. Thank you so much for giving me an opportunity to read this wonderful account of your missionary life in Viet Nam. I do feel like I know you even better now that I have read your book.

INTRODUCTION

F or many years I have thought about writing a book. Each time I would speak, people would ask me when I would write my book. But I am basically an oral storyteller speaker and resisted the discipline, time, and revisions necessary to produce a quality piece of work. Then several things coincided to propel me into motion.

First, I learned of the big celebration occurring in 2011 in both Vietnam and the United States to commemorate the one hundredth anniversary of the entrance of the Gospel—the Good News, or Tin Lanh—to Vietnam. That was a target.

Second, we became "snowbirds" and moved to Shell Point Retirement Community in Fort Myers, Florida for our winters. There, many people are writing memoirs or books in their area of expertise. Woody was privileged to proofread a manuscript by Mali missionary veteran Rosalys Tyler, who wanted to get her experiences in print for family, friends, and co-workers before it was too late. She was 94 when she began this wonderful record. I realized I am in the "age group" where I need to get going on a book to get it off my "bucket list." If it is only for my family and others who faithfully followed us in prayer, that will be enough validation.

Third, whenever we speak about our life in Vietnam, we have people who still tell us they wish members of their family who served in the military there could hear our talk. Even though the country and people of Vietnam have put the war totally behind them, it is still a deep wound in the American psyche. This book is in no way a political treatise, but if these stories can lend meaning, reality, and even humor, to some who served there, I would feel very fulfilled.

Last, and most important, I awoke suddenly at 5:00 a.m. one day in January, 2010 with a compelling thought that I should start my book NOW. I got up and immediately wrote the "things that would have to happen" to get it started; the outline for the book; five goals for each chapter; and a timeline for the development. In fact, I felt a strong sense of destiny and calling. When Woody got up, I shared this with him and received his 100% support which has never flagged. Each of the other "things" happened within a few days, so I began this task with confidence and joy.

I want to say a word to the colleagues who served before us and with us in Vietnam. Please understand that I am not setting myself up as the "ultimate missionary." I am sharing stories that happened to me, and when they include colleagues, I put them in the story. This does not mean I am telling the whole story, only our part. If you find things in the book which you feel are not accurate, please let me know. The stories are not necessarily exactly chronological, but Part I happened during our "first term" and Part II happened during our "second term." When the chapters are about a person, for the most part I have checked that chapter with the person named. Thank you for taking this as a collection of true stories, and not a treatise on missiology.

I want to say a word to any Vietnamese who read this. Please understand that I never want to diminish or disparage your wonderful culture. I may even have misinterpreted or misrepresented it in my stories. In any case, this was not meant in that way. I have attempted to show how a person of another culture tries to "walk into your world" and where it was hard, or funny, or really touching. Without exception, the Pastors and Church members extended great grace to us, loved us, and welcomed us in all our naiveté. We became true colleagues in every sense of the word, and sharing His love with each other was a great witness for sharing God's love to others with you. I have had Vietnamese friends check this manuscript for possible material offensive to you, or incorrect in interpretation, and have made any suggested corrections. I hope that you enjoy reading the stories as much as I have enjoyed telling them.

I sought several opinions about the spelling of the country name. *Viet Nam,* two words, is the original name and was used to describe a species of bird "Viet" in the south "Nam". "Viet" also means to excel, to surpass. *Vietnam,* one word, is now the accepted form for international use. Since the book is in English, I have made it consistent throughout the manuscript in one word. Both ways are right, in case you wondered.

At first, I determined not to have photos in the book; "graphics" are expensive. Then, I thought I would have one picture per chapter. Well, as you can see, I had a very hard time choosing just one most of the time. One of the great joys of preparing the book has been looking at my extensive photo albums of the Vietnam days. Please remember that these are pre-digital photos; most of them are thirty- five years old or more. I hope each one adds "a thousand words" to the stories.

Woody and I have agreed that one dollar from each book that is sold will go toward a scholarship fund at the new Vietnamese Bible School in Ho Chi Minh City.

If anyone wants to talk further about the experiences in this book, I would be more than happy to make an appointment to do that. I dream that it will bring back good memories to many, heal some memories for others, and give glory to God who sent us and kept us during those turbulent years in Vietnam.

Charlotte Stemple stemples@aol.com
Beulah Beach, Vermilion, Ohio
Shell Point Retirement Community, Fort Myers, Florida

DEDICATION

This book is dedicated to the Leadership, Pastors, and People of the Evangelical Church of Viet Nam (Hoi Thanh Tin Lanh Viet Nam) in Viet Nam and the United States and all around the world.

On the occasion of the celebration of the one hundredth anniversary of the entrance of the Good News to Viet Nam, we express our love and appreciation to you in the words of the Apostle Paul in I Thessalonians 1:2-3:

"We always thank God for all of you, mentioning you in our prayers. We continually remember before our God and Father your work produced by faith, your labor prompted by love, and your endurance inspired by hope in our Lord Jesus Christ."

Thank you for accepting and loving us, as you did with all our colleagues, and may God use the Vietnamese believers everywhere to bring many others to faith. We are truly ONE IN CHRIST JESUS.

PART ONE

QUANG NGAI

Woody and Charlotte Stemple

CHAPTER ONE

BEGINNINGS

February 17, 1965. Another beautiful sunny day in Danang, Vietnam. I stood on a hill overlooking the China Sea, attending the funeral of a believer at the little Christian cemetery. As a new language student, I strained desperately to understand some of the strange words and customs when my attention was distracted by a series of boats appearing over the waves in Danang Bay below me. As they neared the shore, these landing craft let down their bay doors and disgorged hundreds of fully equipped military personnel. They were, in fact, American Marines. To my surprise, people began appearing on Red Beach to welcome them: Vietnamese military personnel, girls with sheaves of flower bouquets. and public officials with big smiles and handshakes. Yes, the Marines had landed, and the course of the war, American military history, and our lives would, from this moment, change.

Woody and I had lived in Danang, a city of about 350,000 on the central coast of Vietnam, since the previous October. Deployed as missionaries with the Christian and Missionary Alliance denomination, we joined about eighty others in a country where our coworkers and those before them had served since 1911. They had established many churches called *Tin Lanh* or "Good News" churches throughout the north and the south and had trained leaders and produced the Scripture in Vietnamese. Since the partitioning of Vietnam in 1954, all of our workers were scattered in the south, working both with the Vietnamese people as well as many of the ethnic minorities in the highlands. Actually, Danang was the first place the missionaries had permission to enter; it was then called *Tourane* and was an important port of French Indochina. We now lived on the same piece of land granted to those first workers, in a large, cool, French-style duplex set aside for language students. Because the C&MA believed in learning and living as closely to the people as we could, we were committed to Vietnamese language study for our first year.

Our first month in Danang was historic and horrific; a typhoon, followed by the worst flood in eighty years, ravaged the countryside, and thousands of people died. Our coworkers, Orrel and Gini Steinkamp, who lived in the house next to us, spent countless hours aiding flood victims, hosting members of relief organizations, and taking people to hospitals. Each day we drove down to the Bach Dang River and saw it overflowing its banks, carrying off furniture, houses, logs, dead animals, and sometimes people. Helicopters hovered overhead trying to rescue people, and we came to understand that this was not a "normal" rainy season. Orrel and Gini spent long hours with the church leaders helping the homeless, the hurting, and the hungry. The rain poured incessantly: we felt helpless and permanently chilled, and no one had time to find us a language helper.

After a few weeks, as things settled down, two young people were engaged to teach us Vietnamese: a young woman for me and a young man for Woody. We had a textbook with words and phrases and sat each day at separate desks in our apartment for four to six hours while Co Binh and Anh Mai spoke elementary words to us and we repeated them over and over and over. Thankfully, a few centuries earlier a French Jesuit priest created a Roman based alphabet for the Vietnamese language; this eventually became the national written language of Vietnam in the 20ᵗʰ century replacing the Chinese-based pictograms. Each written word has up to six different tone marks, so we not only learned the word, but also the tone that went with it. Yes, that made it "easy" to read since it was phonetically regular, but we had no idea what we were hearing, saying, or meaning!

Vietnamese is basically monosyllabic, but oh, that one syllable! For example, *ma* could be said six different ways and each way had a totally unrelated meaning...such as horse, grave, but, mother, ghost. A wrong tone totally destroyed the meaning, and puzzled looks followed half of our attempts at conversation.

There were a lot of snags in our language learning system. For one thing, in Vietnamese culture it is not proper for a younger person to correct an older one, especially not someone as prestigious as a minister. So, as we faithfully repeated our words and phrases, our teachers nodded their heads and smiled. They never told us we were murdering half the words, and by the time our "seniors" came to check up, we had managed to learn a lot of bad habits. We tried just to learn to say "Hello" or "Hi" but to our dismay, it's not that simple in Vietnamese. One has to know the gender, age, relationship, and profession of someone to say hello, because hello is always followed by a word of address such as child, sir, old lady, teacher, pastor or some other definitive description. Also, we did not know there are eight ways you can have an uncle or an aunt; and each has a different name in this great language. Furthermore, one doesn't just "carry" something; there are about seven descriptive ways to do it. This is made very clear once you learn the words, but causes a lot of laughs before you do, such as saying you are carrying your baby slung over your shoulder.

Learning our numbers made us bold enough to go shopping in the market, but the bargaining system almost got the better of us until we learned what an enjoyable game it is for all concerned and took our early losses in good stride. Every conversation had pitfalls, and we had to keep checking with each other to be sure we were hearing the same thing. Finally, after we declared it was 'vomiting' outside (instead of raining) and that I was giving birth in the guest room (instead of painting it), we learned the biggest lesson of all; to laugh at ourselves and enjoy their amusement — and their happiness that we were making an effort.

However, we did learn, often by rote, which was the preferred learning style in Vietnam. As soon as Woody memorized the benediction, they called on him at every service to say it. What a joy we felt when we could hear and find the hymn numbers as they were announced, and what great success we experienced in following along with the sermon in church in our Vietnamese Bible. Today I can still say grace at meals, pray for the sick, and recite the Lord's Prayer, the twenty-third Psalm, and the Apostle's Creed. Not to mention . . . give a message, order food in a restaurant, recite poetry, carry on a long conversation and tell jokes in this beautiful descriptive language.

But we soon realized that language learning was really the least of our worries. The culture almost did us in. For one thing, the Vietnamese have a different view of personal space and privacy. Sometimes our teachers, bored with repeating the same phrases would look through our desk drawers, read our mail, use our hairspray, or ask us about a personal item they would discover.

Perfectly acceptable questions on first acquaintance included "How old are you?" "How much do you weigh?" "What did that cost?" "How much do you make?" and "How many children do you have?" We learned to proudly give our age; say we weighed less than a sack of rice; that an item cost more than what we wanted to pay; and that actually we were volunteers. When we said we had no children yet, we got the stumper, "Whose fault is it, yours or your husband's?" So we learned a useful theological phrase, "It's God's fault."

Then there were the names . . . every person's name had at least three parts. Their first name was their family name, or what we would call their "last name." A girl's middle name was always *thi*. A boy's middle name was usually the same as his father's. Then the third name was the given name. It is a wonderful system because you can distinguish who belongs to whom, since there are a limited number of family names. Of course, we had an awful time saying the most common family name, Nguyen, because English does not use the *ng* sound at the beginning of a word. But we paid them back since Vietnamese does not use the *st* diphthong at the beginning of the word, and over the course of five years they were faced with missionaries named Stebbins, Steinkamp, Stemple, and Stedman. But actually it didn't matter to them because they called us all Mr. and Mrs. Missionary, the proper way to address us in their language.

Two incidents that first year caused us to seriously reconsider our call to Vietnam. The first was the traumatic murder of English missionary, John Haywood, as he traveled across the Hai Van Pass between Danang and Hue. This was a common and safe trip for civilians and it was never determined who shot him or why. Although from another mission, he and his Swiss wife, Simone, and small daughter, Jacqueline, were good friends of ours and this seemingly senseless act was difficult to comprehend. We all questioned if violence against civilians would escalate.

About that same time, our mission sent a letter to all our missionaries asking for us to reply to this hypothetical question: If the conditions escalate in Vietnam and civilians are asked to leave the country, name two countries where you would be willing to be redeployed. We called our mis-

sion office immediately. "If you think we are going to have
to leave," we said, "we are not going to spend another day
trying to learn this language." We sent back the letter with
the countries of Mali and Argentina named—for no good
reason at all. "Rex" Rexilius, our mission vice chairman
came from Saigon to calm us down assuring us that it was
just a formality; he believed we would have at least ten good
years to serve in Vietnam. That was prophetic!

Just when we needed it, we got an unexpected change
of pace for a day. A few weeks before Christmas, a U.S.
Chaplain told us that Bob Hope, the great American enter-
tainer, was coming to Danang and he could get us precious
tickets to see the show. Orrel and Gini Steinkamp and I were
the chosen ones. On the appointed day, we went to the big
airbase very early and were admitted. Thousands of GIs
poured in and sat right on the tarmac before the big stage in
front of an airplane hangar which had a tent inside for the
performers. Well, we got right next to the side of the stage
toward the back and had a great side view.

As we waited for the show to start, a military policeman
came up to us and said, "I am sorry, but Mr. Hope has chosen
this show as his annual Christmas television special *Bob
Hope with the Troops,* and people will wonder who you two
women are, so Mr. Hope has asked that I escort you to the
back of the audience." Yes, we were almost the only women
present and this was very disappointing . . . and embarrassing
. . . but we meekly went along. As we came to the back of the
crowd the Colonel, head of the air base, came running over
to us and said, "I am so glad to see you. The women need
someone to help them in the dressing tent, and I didn't know
who to ask . . . will you help?" Of course we would! (I know
there were 10,000 men there who would have been glad to
help also!) He escorted us to the tent, where we met and
shook hands with Bob Hope, and entered to see six gorgeous
women trying to get their act together. The Colonel intro-

duced us to each one including Miss World, Anne Sydney from England, so I can actually say I stood next to the most beautiful woman in the world.

The tent dressing room brimmed with commotion. When we asked how we could help, Annamaria Alberghetti asked if we had an iron. "No", we said, "we are sorry we can't help with that." In fact, we didn't even know if there was electricity there. She asked Gini to hold her dress high and shake it slightly until she needed to put it on, which thankfully was only a few minutes later. Local vendors measured them for shoe sizes so they could give the girls gifts. They ran into a problem since the beautiful pre-cut lacquered soles were all size five and under, so they ended up presenting the girls with the typical cone-shaped Vietnamese hats instead. Jill St.John was trying to zip herself into a form-fitting gold lame dress and I offered to help. "Oh no," she replied, "no one touches this zipper." She then expertly hooked a hanger-like wire into the end of the zipper and quickly sheathed herself into it.

There really wasn't a lot more we could do as we watched them add wigs and apply makeup. Pretty soon Les Brown and his Band of Renown started playing, and the girls thanked us and went running out to go on stage and do their thing. So Gini and I looked at each other and said we might as well go out and see what's happening.

The Colonel thanked us profusely and then asked us where we planned to sit. Confessing that we had no seat, he informed us that there were chairs right in front of the platform that we could have, so he led us, tripping over everyone, straight to the front row while Orrel watched round-eyed from his now second-rate, stage side position. We wrote home, "Watch the Bob Hope Show this Christmas. The two beauties in the front row seats are your missionaries in action." We were living proof of "the last shall be first!"

And it was a great show, even if it didn't really fit into our annual report anywhere.

Gradually, in spite of it all, we began to learn the language, survive the heat, get adjusted in our own little apartment, and build relationships and eventually good friendships with individuals and young couples. I had gotten into a great daily routine. Each day we would study with our teacher from 9:00-12:00 then have lunch, our noon rest (when everything shut down including schools, shops, public offices), and then more study from 2:00-4:00 when we finally had our freedom. My coworker Gini and I would get on our bicycles, pedal down the beautiful wide flame-tree bordered boulevards to the post office to pick up the mission mail. There we would elbow our way to the window to buy needed stamps or supplies. We would then head for the Air Vietnam office to weigh ourselves on the baggage scales . . . followed by a stop at the ice cream shop for our daily treat. Finally, we would head home for supper, which was prepared by our helper, followed by more study, letters, and bed.

Yes, there were days that first year we thought we might as well go home, but many people prayed for us and their prayers were heard and answered. Just before our one-year exam, I did it. I dreamed in Vietnamese. They say that is a mark of learning a language. I think I was just cramming for the exam, which we both passed.

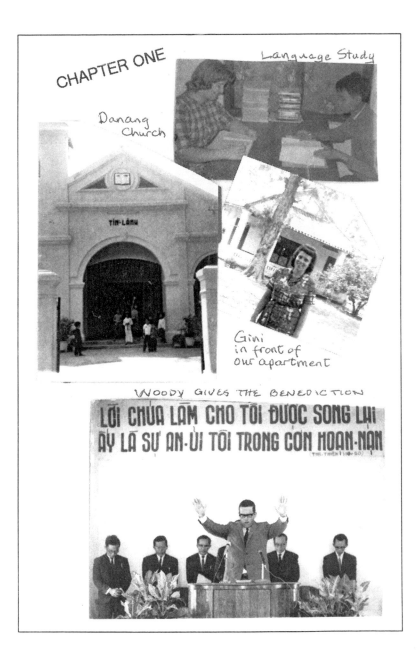

CHAPTER ONE

Language Study

Danang Church

Gini in front of our apartment

WOODY GIVES THE BENEDICTION

Rescuing villagers in flooded town

A million persons were left homeless and thousands were drowned

1964
Danang

Worst flood
in 80 years

The girls in the show: Miss World,
Ann Sydney; Anita Bryant; Janis Paige;
Annamaria Alberghetti; Jill St. John
and of course, Bob Hope himself.

Part of the huge crowd out on the strip
Note Dillard family and TWO EMPTY SEATS
in front of them where Gini and I sat
later after helping dress the girls!

Can you see the empty chairs?

CHAPTER TWO

SISTER TEN

W e had a house helper, much to our dismay at first. We left the United States as children of the sixties; not radicals, of course, but feeling very independent, influenced by the civil rights movement and ready to change the world. Added to our Biblical beliefs about the dignity of each individual and God's love for him/her as well as social justice and care for the poor, we were horrified at the thought that we were expected to have "house help." Not to mention that we got a "living allowance" and not a "salary" from our mission; we never dreamed of putting house help into our budget . . . no one we knew at home had a maid. A BIG cultural insight was coming.

First, we found out that the young woman they had already engaged for us had worked for every couple who had studied language in our house for several years. If we *refused* to hire her, she would lose face tremendously in her community since no one would believe our reasons and think there must be something about her that was undesirable. Second, we learned that a *servant* in their culture was expected at every level of society, and that the more prominent a person you worked for, the higher your own reputation. A quick review of scripture showed us that Abraham's servant (who would have inherited his wealth if he had no sons) and Elijah's servant were trusted advisers and had high social standing. Even our helper had a young girl working for her to care for her young children while she worked for us.

Furthermore, in those days it was necessary to get water from a well for washing in our washhouse, or for bathing in our big indoor tin tub . . . and if you wanted hot water, you had to build a fire and heat it. We did have running water for our toilets and sinks, but to drink it, you had to boil the water for twenty minutes and run it through a stone filter. Due to the heat, we had to wash and bathe often and, of course, drink LOTS of water. To fix meals, market shopping had to be done daily and vegetables had to be carefully prepared, often by soaking in purple potassium permanganate. Buying meat was no simple chore as it hung on the shop hooks ready to be cut to order. Vietnamese market sellers cut the meat so differently from American butchers, often whacking a chicken into many puzzling parts with their cleavers. Cooking was all done from scratch (no quick mixes) and every recipe I had would need to have some equivalent substitute figured out. Also, because we lived behind the market, we needed to dust and mop the tile floors daily. Bottom line, JUST TO LIVE would take us eight hours a day and leave no time or energy for study.

And . . . there were no such things as "fixed hours." Chi Muoi would come when we needed her, fix all our meals, go home for a nap while we had our siesta hour, and take Sundays off . . . unless we needed her. Her wages would be a whopping $17.00 per month; within our budget! So, it wasn't rationalization, but realization . . . we were now in Vietnam and I would have house help. But I never could call her a servant.

Actually, we would not have made it without Chi Muoi. Her name meant "Older Sister, Number Ten." In Vietnam no

one is ever just called a name; the name always has to have
sister, brother, teacher, or something in front of it. Because
she was a bit older, and we were to be like family, she was
"older sister." And because she was the ninth child in a
family, she was called number ten. The Vietnamese have a
great way of designating the often numerous children in a
family. They begin counting with number two (way back in
time it was to keep the evil spirits from snatching or harming
the first child so they did not call any child "Number One.")
The habit persists but not the belief, and each child is "numbered" even though they are also given a regular name. All
through their lifetime they are known to their family as
"Sister Seven" or "Brother Four," and known to the public
by their given name.

Chi Muoi became like a sister to me. From the beginning
when we had no words to communicate, she demonstrated
how to cut and clean the food, find things in the market,
store groceries so the mice or ants would not get into them,
keep the house cool, and use chopsticks. She always had
cold drinks ready for us when we took our language breaks.
I was her "boss" but she gave us tips on many cultural dos
and don'ts. For example, we learned that as soon as a guest
comes into the house he is to be seated and offered something to drink. If this does not take place within five minutes
of entry, a guest feels unwelcome. So when anyone dropped
into our apartment, we whisked him or her immediately to
the chair beside the small center coffee table where the teaset
sat waiting to greet the visitor. I also learned that the more
expensive the tea, the smaller the teacup; so I was actually
honored when I only got a thimbleful of tea. Over the years
we would be in Vietnam, I never entered a home, large or
small, from that of the province chief to a poor cardboard
refugee hut, without being offered something to drink. It was
usually tea, but often Coca Cola or Fanta, with or without
ice.

When Chi Muoi first began working for us we were still in our naïve American mode and tried to get her to sit down and eat with us instead of standing in the kitchen and waiting for us to finish so she could do the dishes. One time we insisted so much that she sat down and we served her a plate. She hunched over, put her head in her hands, and did not move until we finished our meal; then she quietly took our empty plates and her full one to the kitchen, brought us our dessert and resumed her stance in the kitchen. We finally realized it would be like asking the waitress in the local restaurant to join you at the table and eat; this was just not the way it worked.

Chi Muoi had learned from others how to cook wonderful American food from Vietnamese fresh products. One night she made a great meatloaf supper and as we were eating Woody got up and went to the refrigerator to get the ketchup. About five minutes later, our colleagues came from the other house with Chi Muoi leading them and crying. As they came in, we jumped up and asked, "What is the matter?" They said, "Chi Muoi wants to know why you don't like her anymore?" "Like her?" we said, "we LOVE her; we couldn't be here without her. Why does she think we don't like her?" After some consultation, they told us, "You don't like her because Mr. Missionary (Woody) got up and got his own ketchup and didn't allow her to do it." OH MY! For one thing, we didn't know the word for ketchup. And, where we came from, if you asked someone to go get you ketchup, they might ask, "Who broke your leg?" Peace was restored.

Chi Muoi was small, timid, and very humble in her behavior, but strong in her faith and very loving. It was Chi Muoi who cared for me when I had a miscarriage that first year. It happened very suddenly one night when I was still early in my pregnancy, but it was very painful and traumatic. We were heartbroken as this was the fourth failed attempt at having the children we so desperately wanted; previously I had two miscarriages and one ruptured ectopic pregnancy. Woody did his best to comfort me, but we had to wait until morning to get any medical help, and the night seemed long and lonely. In the morning Chi Muoi drew water and heated it, carried it to the tin tub, and lovingly washed me as I wept.

I received medical help from a friendly American doctor who worked at the Vietnamese civilian hospital. He slipped me in ahead of everyone in line and gave me a brief examination. He then gave me the choice of being cared for by him immediately without anesthesia right there, or waiting for a minor surgery slot the next day and having a poorly trained student do anesthesia. A choice? I took the immediate. What followed is unprintable. Let's just say I screamed. All the Vietnamese were trying to see in, and the doctor kept saying, "I thought missionaries were supposed to endure hardship like good soldiers of Jesus." When I staggered out of that room, I think most of the waiting line had run away. Woody tenderly took me home and Chi Muoi made me *chao ga*, the wonderful chicken-rice porridge that makes everything better.

The biggest challenge Chi Muoi and I had was attempting to keep our house bug free; together we had lots of tricks to take care of the problems. Woody and I slept under mosquito nets at night; she put the legs of our screened-in food cupboards in bowls of water to keep out the ants; we sprayed and kept things covered, and we set traps. We learned to love the little geckos that were always scurrying around on the walls; they kept down our "other-bug" population. We would hear their little squeaky mating calls and watch where they disappeared. We discovered their hiding places and found their "maternity ward" behind our big picture on the dining room wall. But they always seemed to know their place and leave us alone. That left only one problem: cockroaches. Even Chi Muoi could not help with those.

I am from the northern U.S., so cockroaches always equaled "dirt" to me. In fact, I had never seen one in any home I had ever lived in, but now I was faced with them from day one. Not many, but they were BIG. When I opened my drawers, they scurried away out of sight; when I threw something in the trash, I uncovered them; when I would pull open a cupboard I would see them cowering at the back. Worse yet, they left their little black ovoid "calling cards" everywhere. Then, at certain times, they would *swarm* or fly out of everywhere and find a new hiding place. I was freaked out. At each scream when I would come upon one, Woody would say, "What's the problem? Did you notice they are scurrying AWAY from you?" or, "What's the problem? You are a lot bigger than they are!" Delivering me from either the cockroaches or my fears became my chief prayer request.

When I finally told Gini, our colleague, how distraught I was, she offered me some paper to line my kitchen cupboards and drawers which she promised would absolutely get rid of them. When she gave me one of her precious rolls, within minutes, I was back home taking care of the situation. AND IT WORKED. I never saw a cockroach in any place I had put the paper. I never knew or cared what chemistry or calamity was happening to those bugs, I just knew it worked.

Within a few weeks I wrote a letter of commendation to the bug paper company. I told them how effective their product was and asked them to send me a <u>case</u> of paper and I would pay them whatever it cost. A few weeks later, I got word that a case was on its way to me and it would be free if I would allow them to use my letter in their advertising. The sample ad they sent me to endorse started with the huge headline: "WE WIN THE WAR IN VIETNAM." It went on, "Mrs. Charlotte Stemple of Danang Vietnam writes us, your product is the only thing we have found that is effective against our cockroaches..." I gave them full permission, reported to our headquarters that I would be endorsing a product, used the complete case of paper with great joy, had my sanity restored, and never knew if the ad ever went to print or not. How ridiculous it seemed within a few years that bugs had even been a big issue for me.

Yes, the cultural adaptations were many, but the person and presence of Sister Ten made a huge difference for us that Year One in Vietnam.

Chị Mười
SISTER TEN

CHAPTER THREE

FRIEND BETTY

As more and more American units came to Vietnam, and Danang specifically, we got to know many fine military personnel. We were still immersed in six-hour-a-day language study and full church activities and visits, but it was a welcome break for us to be able to speak English and *see* Danang from a different perspective. Many chaplains came to visit to learn how they could help the Vietnamese people (and maybe to get off the base and visit a family for awhile). Their generosity was expressed in countless sponsored projects all over Vietnam throughout their tours of duty. Vietnam was always a "remote" location, so no families accompanied the troops; in the beginning years there were no female troops and the men lived at war readiness.

The GIs were seldom allowed off-base except in a controlled environment and considered all Vietnamese potential enemies. We eagerly showed them the wonderful family of believers in our many churches in the Danang area; one church and school sat exactly at the end of the airbase runway, and the large Danang church and parsonage were just across our driveway.

Because the Vietnamese had no services on Sunday evenings, and we had no responsibilities then, we and our colleagues coordinated with some Chaplains to have a service at the airbase every Sunday evening called "Country Church." Gini played the organ and we sang old fashioned Gospel songs with great vigor. Some of the military guys would give testimonies and one of the missionaries would preach. The small English-speaking community and their families would come and it became very popular with the airmen and eventually GIs from all the bases around Danang, regardless of service unit or even religious affiliation. It was a real touch of home.

On uniquely American holidays, like Thanksgiving and New Year's Day, we usually had all the U.S. civilian personnel (3 or 4 families from other missions) and some of the servicemen over for potluck and flag football in the little yard on our property. Vietnamese do not value "grass" as it becomes a place of refuse along the streets, so it is considered a weed. They pull all greenery, pack down the dirt, and use potted plants for decorating their yards. They have very nice shrubs and hedges, and take great pride in their property, but in the city most houses are built right on the street; often with shops or businesses on the first floor and living quarters above. So, our little protected square of grass was cut by hand by our yard worker and enjoyed as an oasis or a mini-ballfield by American visitors. The men from the base supplied us with many holiday treats since they could buy such goodies at the well-stocked PX; how ironic that our Christmas wrapping paper, trees, decorations, and specialty foods were often better in Danang than they had been at home, due to the generosity of the GIs.

As more troops came, the military opened a USO building downtown as a getaway for troops; they served hamburgers and milkshakes, had pool and ping pong tables, and a movie room. But they had no USO women to help, so they recruited the missionary women for Saturdays. We flipped the burgers, talked with the guys, and encouraged or helped them write home (long before e-mails or even phone calls were possible). We even got called "Doughnut Dollies," which is apparently a World War II designation for USO women workers. It was funny how many wives and mothers were amazed and delighted (and usually unbelieving) to hear their husbands or sons were spending time with missionaries! By this time we had a single woman language student who had joined us in the apartments in Danang and she also joined us at the USO. It changed the dynamics a bit to have Betty along and we had a lot of fun with that, to Betty's consternation.

One week a well-known American syndicated columnist met Betty in our downtown Danang USO building. He was quite taken with her dedication to medical missions, specifically to those with Hansen's disease (leprosy) and titled his article, "Betty, the Belle of Danang." He wrote a flattering column about the red-haired, green-eyed, lissome lovely with the unshakeable calling whom he had met at the USO. Soon Betty began getting letters from all over the U.S. as her "prayer warriors" in women's groups were quite perplexed at this description and workplace for the Betty they sent off to do God's work! We really got a laugh as she got a telegram from the Paris *Match* magazine asking to do a photo spread of her on China Beach. We encouraged her to send it to our national headquarters for permission, but she was not amused.

I actually had known Betty for some years before her arrival in Vietnam, meeting her during my time as a student at Nyack College in New York. She had completed her nurses' training and I took over after her as nurse in the Boys' Dorm at Simpson Hall. Betty was born in 1934 and raised in West Africa, the daughter of missionaries. By the time I met her, she was very bitter about circumstances in her life and struggling emotionally. She vowed she would "never be a missionary" and that it was no way to live and bring up a family. She was acerbic in conversation; cutting and curt in remarks she made to other people, including me. I lost track of her when she left Nyack.

When we had been studying about half a year in Danang, our colleagues, Orrel and Gini, told us that another language student would be joining us and her name was Betty Olsen. Woody and I looked at each other; it could NOT be the same person we knew; certainly it was a common name. But when she arrived, it WAS the same Betty Olsen, only not "the same" at all.

Betty told us that she had gone to Chicago to work as a nurse totally defeated as a Christian and unhappy with life in general. Her deep depression even caused her to consider suicide, but then she was greatly helped by interaction with her church counselor named Bill Gothard. She would even go on to work for Bill who conducted the very popular and successful Institute in Basic Youth Conflicts, based greatly on his work with Betty. During this time, she recognized her calling and gave her life to spend with Vietnamese tribal leprous peoples. However, she first had to do the obligatory year of Vietnamese language study, so she moved into the apartment next to us.

Betty and I became close friends; she was still a bit abrupt in conversation, but we spent long hours discussing concepts like forgiveness, grace, disappointment and marriage. She was greatly influenced by the writings of Madame Jeanne Guyon—a French mystic from the early 1700s—and told me how Madame Guyon had forgiven her husband and mother-in-law for putting her in prison and terribly mistreating her for her faith. This was to be a good lesson for Betty.

After our year of language study we moved to Quang Ngai province to work with the Vietnamese and Betty moved to the mountain town of Banmethuot where she would work in a leprosarium and learn the language of the people she now lived among, the Raday. She came to spend Christmas with us in 1967, rejoicing in our infant son Stewart and telling us about the life she was now living and loving. When we talked about the heightened war situation, Betty remarked, "Well, God called me to come to Vietnam; He didn't say anything about going back."

Two months later, during the Tet offensive of 1968, when six Alliance missionaries lost their lives in Banmethuot, Betty was taken captive during the attacks on the mission compound as she courageously tried to secure medications for the wounded. Hank Blood, a Wycliffe missionary, and Mike Benge, a U.S. Aid worker, were also captured with her. For the next month or so, Benge, Blood and Betty were held in a POW camp in Darlac Province, about a day's walk from Banmethuot. They were held in cages where they had nothing to eat but boiled *manioc*. The Vietnamese kept moving their prisoners; hiking through the jungles and mountains. The camp areas, swept very clean of leaves to keep the mosquito population down, were clearly visible from the air. Once, Benge reports, an American aircraft came so close to the camp that he could see the pilot's face. The pilot 'wagged his wings' and flew away. The Vietnamese, fearing rescue attempts and U.S. air strikes, kept moving.

For months, Olsen, Blood, and Benge were chained together and moved north from one encampment to another, moving over 200 miles through the mountainous jungles. The trip was grueling and took its toll on the prisoners. They were physically depleted, sick from dysentery and malnutrition; beset by fungus, infection, leeches, and ulcerated sores. Mike Benge contracted cerebral malaria and nearly died. He credits Betty Olsen with keeping him alive. She forced him to rouse from his delirium to eat and drink water and rice soup. Mike Benge describes Betty as "a Katherine Hepburn type . . . with an extra bit of grit."

In the summer of 1968, the prisoners, again on the trail, were left exposed to the rain during the rainy season. Hank Blood contracted pneumonia, weakened steadily, and eventually died in July. He was buried in a shallow grave along the trail; Betty conducted the graveside service. Benge and Olsen were kept moving. Their bodies were covered with sores and they had pyorrhea from beriberi, a severe vitamin deficiency. Their teeth were loosening and gums infected. They were forced to move every two to three days, through at least three provinces. Betty weakened and the Vietnamese began to kick and drag her to keep her moving. Mike, trying to defend her, was beaten with rifle butts.

Just before crossing the border into Cambodia, Betty weakened to the point that she could no longer move. Ironically, in this area, near a tributary to the Mekong River, fish and livestock abounded and there was a garden but the food was denied to the prisoners. Their captors allowed them to gather bamboo shoots but they were not told how to cook them. Bamboo needs to be boiled in two waters to extract an acid substance. Not knowing this, Betty and Mike boiled their food only once and were beset with immobilizing stomach cramps within a half hour; diarrhea soon followed. Betty weakened further and finally died September 29, 1968; Mike Benge buried her in the jungle.

Mike Benge endured more grueling captivity both in Cambodia and Vietnam for over three years, including twenty-seven months in solitary confinement. When released, he reported on and verified the deaths of Hank Blood and Betty Olsen. When talking about Betty, he expressed amazement at her loving and forgiving attitude to her captors; in fact, her life and death along the Ho Chi Minh trail made a profound difference in his own life and outlook on eternity.

Ironically, Betty had mailed a thank you letter to us after her Christmas visit and before the Tet Holiday. It was sent via the Vietnamese postal service but we did not receive it until about May of that year. On the outside of the envelope was an official stamp which said "Mail delivery delayed due to wartime conditions." Inside Betty had written at the end of the note, "Have a good Tet. Don't let the VC get you." Oh, friend Betty, they didn't "get you" either!!

Source for some of this material: Homecoming II Project, June 30, 1990, compiled from one or more of the following: raw data from U.S. Government agency sources, correspondence with POW/MIA families, published sources, interviews.

CHAPTER THREE

FRIEND BETTY & STEWART

AP Wirephoto

Betty Olsen

Sisters -- Betty and Binh Minh

The Evening Bulletin 27

PHILADELPHIA, Friday, May 7, 1965   B

Da Nang Belle Shuns Dates With GIs; She's a Missionary

By HAL BOYLE

Da Nang, South Viet Nam, May 7—(AP)—To airmen and marines, she's the Belle of Da Nang.

Miss Betty Olsen, 30, a medical missionary, takes the nickname as a pleasant joke.

"I think I'm the only single girl here," she said, "but there are a number of married women in our mission."

Many an American girl would think it a dream situation to be the only girl amid 10,000 men. But Betty, who is tall and slender and has auburn hair and green eyes, is more amused than thrilled.

A USO Volunteer

Every Saturday morning she serves as a volunteer worker at the United Service Organization in the heart of the city. Many of the men have asked for a date, but each has met with a refusal.

"They are all nice and polite," said Miss Olsen. "If they want to be friends, that's fine. But I don't date them. I am not interested in romance, and I have no idea of getting married."

She is deeply religious woman whose goal since childhood has been to do medical missionary work. She was born in Africa and both her parents are missionaries on Africia's Ivory Coast.

Learns the Language

Betty was educated at New York Missionary College and studied nursing at the Methodist Hospital in Brooklyn. She was sent here last December by the Christian and Missionary Alliance, which has 900 missionaries in 24 foreign countries.

She attends six religious meetings weekly and spends two nights a week teaching English to a group of 60 Vietnamese.

"Most of them are teenagers but a few are older," she said. "They are very interested and eager to learn.

"They are particularly curious about America. I told them about the skyscrapers and the subways but I am afraid they didn't understand subways or why anyone would want them.

"They also wanted me to compare New York and Da Nang, and that was a little difficult, too.

"The Vietnamese people I have met are very friendly to Americans and say they are glad our men are here."

Plans to Stay

Although she gets a little homesick, Betty says she plans to spend her life in Viet Nam. She hopes to work in a leprosarium in the interior. But, that area now is largely controlled by the Communist Viet Cong guerillas.

"I like it here and I am quite happy," Betty said. "It makes me feel at home because the climate and the tropical foliage remind me of Africa. My parents are happy, too, that I was called to this work."

Does she ever feel uneasy at being in a war zone?

"God called me to be a missionary," she said. "I have no fear, because I know I am in the center of God's will."

CHAPTER FOUR

WHERE NEXT ?

A s we neared the end of our language learning year in
Danang, we had the privilege of deciding where in
Vietnam we wanted to serve. The mission field leadership
team would have to approve, and the national church with
whom we worked would need to be consulted. Up until
we arrived in Vietnam, missionaries who came were pre-
assigned to either the Tribal minorities or the Vietnamese
people. We were the first to have a choice and we had no
clue which way to go. We, and our many friends and family,
were praying for guidance in our decision. Our colleagues
outlined to us the advantages of each side.

Our friends and co-workers, Roy and Nancy Josephsen,
worked among the Bru minority people in the northwest
corner of South Vietnam in a little village called Khe Sanh,
later to be the site of one of the greatest battles of the Vietnam
conflict. They wanted us to join them, so Roy arranged a trip
there in an Army Caribou airplane to allow us to see the village and meet some people. The fact that there were no safe
roads there should have given us a clue.

Sitting on canvas sling seats and flying with the back
cargo door "open," I thoroughly enjoyed the flight. Roy had
just mentioned that we seemed to be taking a long time to

get there when we heard "ping, ping, ping" like gravel on a newly paved road hitting the bottom of the plane. "Anti-aircraft guns!" the loadmaster yelled as he threw me a flak jacket. "Sit on this," he commanded. The pilot put the plane into a steep climb and turned to fly out of range. After flying about ten minutes Roy said, "There's the Dong Ha River. We have been flying over North Vietnam all this time." We followed the river west to Khe Sanh and landed without further ado. Yes, the pilot later told us he had been given the wrong coordinates and we had flown too far north. There were lots of bullet holes in the plane, but none in vital parts—thank the Lord. Our mission office got another letter from me, this time asking for combat pay. They refused on the grounds we had not had their permission to leave the country.

Our drama did not end there. When we landed in Khe Sanh, the Vietnamese pastor, who also worked with the Bru people, told Roy that the windows and doors for the new church they were building were waiting for air transport from the Dong Ha landing strip. The truck could only get them that far. The accommodating military pilot, with time on his hands, volunteered to go to Dong Ha and bring them back to Khe Sanh. So Roy sent the pastor's wife, and me, with my rudimentary Vietnamese, to go pick up the cargo while he and Woody went to visit the people and see the area of Khe Sanh.

When we got to Dong Ha we got into a very precarious situation. After we located the windows and doors and began loading them on the plane, lots of Vietnamese soldiers, trying also to get to Khe Sanh, began swarming the plane. The pilot was trying to get them to help load, but they were not listening. He pulled a gun and told me to tell them to help load first. I had not exactly learned phrases for this situation so I stood in the plane yelling in my best Vietnamese, "No work, No go, No work, No go, No work, No go" while pointing at the cargo. The pastor's wife was wailing and pointing and praying at the top of her voice. They finally got the idea and loaded the windows and doors and then climbed frantically on top of them as the pilot raced down the runway. We arrived in Khe Sanh with half of the glass broken, but no lives lost.

The rest of the trip went well. Khe Sanh was a typical slow-moving mountain jungle town far from the amenities of civilization. We sat in the pastor's home drinking wonderful coffee, fresh from the nearby plantations, and eating mangos, papaya and bananas. The work was going well and a nice church building was under construction. Good well water was available, the language was being written, and the people were welcoming and friendly. We flew back without incident, but deep down knew this was not God's calling for our lives at this point. In fact, we felt that we had fallen in love with the Vietnamese people and would somehow minister among them. I honestly do not think our reluctance was because we did not want to learn another language, but that might have been a part of it. We still had a long way to go in Vietnamese.

We really relied on verses of Proverbs 3:5, 6 which say, "Trust in the Lord with all your heart, lean not on your own understanding. In all your ways acknowledge Him, and He will direct your paths." That direction came late in the year. An older Vietnamese pastor from Quang Ngai, a province about 150 kilometers south of Danang, came to visit us. We had met him in a group setting but we had never had a conversation with him. We knew the mission had a house in Quang Ngai and former missionaries Duttons, Livingstons and Olivers had lived there, but presently no Americans were there. Route One, the main highway that went from north to south, had been "cut" by the Viet Cong in many places and bridges were bombed out, so we could not visit there by road. The only way in or out to the provinces north or south would be by military plane or by the weekly Air Vietnam flight. So we were glad to have a visit from Pastor Le Chau, even though we were not sure what he wanted.

We soon found out he wanted to recruit us to come to Quang Ngai at the conclusion of language study. He had three compelling reasons why: 1) The war was worse there than any other province and people were dying without Christ. 2) The harvest was ripe there and the workers few: people were coming to him with petitions to bring the Gospel to their area. He pastored the main province center church, and four other country area churches had young or student pastors. They needed us to help "bring in the harvest" as the doors were wide open. 3) Somehow he knew we had difficulty having children; we had experienced four pregnancies which had ended early and badly, so he told us, "If you move to Quang Ngai and drink the water there, you will have children." That convinced us, so we went to Quang Ngai right after Christmas to scope out the situation.

We flew down in a military plane and were met by two single girls from another mission. They were working on translating a tribal language and temporarily living in "our house" so we got to stay there and enjoy a chilly, rainy few days with them. It was a nice cement house right on the main road from town out to the airfield, next to the province hospital and across the road from the Vietnamese military hospital. It had beautiful bougainvillea over the front gate and a small "driveway" where we could leave our car. It also had a well and a water storage tank where we would pump water when we had electricity, or do it by hand. Coconut trees ringed the entire property, including the yard out back. Sugar cane fields flanked us to the side and back, along with a few farm style mud brick homes with thatched roofs.

Inside, our floors were all nicely tiled; we had a living-dining room and three other small rooms. One would become our office/guest room, one our own bedroom, and one the room where we built our required sandbag bunker and, later, the "nursery." The windows were nicely screened and had wooden shutters that we closed each night. They also had metal bars on them to keep out thieves. Our little bathroom had a tub with shower, sink, and a toilet which flushed by pulling a chain on the overhead tank. The very small kitchen had shelves, a *garde-manger* (screened food cupboard), kerosene refrigerator, propane stove, and a sink with cold running water. I loved it.

Like most Vietnamese houses, we stepped down from the kitchen to the well area where much of "life" would take place. Our Vietnamese worker preferred to cook outside, and the neighbors gathered here as they used our well for the good water. A building like a garage held a storeroom, washroom, and a local "squat pot" style bathroom with a large ceramic water reservoir to dip out the rinse and flush water. We parked our car there as well. I couldn't wait to move into this busy neighborhood right in the middle of life in Quang Ngai.

Pastor and Mrs. Le Chau and the elders came to visit and again welcomed us with open arms. The church was about a mile toward town from us, right across the street from the province headquarters and near the central intersection. This is where Route One ran its broken, potholed, bombed- out way from the Mekong Delta in the far south, to Quang Tri on the northern divided border and then on north to Hanoi. Only small portions of the road were open in our province, and none of them connected to anywhere very far away. Our new friends Eva and Jackie showed us around town; they took us down to the river and out toward "Buddha Mountain." They also showed us where to buy food in the market. They made us wonderful meals from local products. Even though it was rainy season and too chilly for the yeast rolls and bread to rise (they put the dough under blankets with hot stones and it still did not work), they tasted wonderful just the same.

After three days, we were convinced God was leading us to Quang Ngai to serve with Pastor Chau in the main province church and with the five other young pastors who had churches out in the countryside. Permission was granted and we permanently moved there the beginning of the year, driving down in stages in our green Volkswagen van (converted from panel van to passenger van) with TIN LANH painted on the side and our stuff packed around us. We never doubted God had brought us there. All of Pastor Le Chau's three reasons for moving there were true, and, above all, they loved us, accepted us, and shared their lives with us.

Our first Sunday in church (with Woody on the front row on the men's side and me on the woman's side), we looked at each other across the room and smiled with joy; finally we were "real missionaries." After singing some hymns, the pastor made an announcement. First, he asked us to stand. Looking at each other, we got it and stood up. Then he welcomed us and introduced us to the congregation. Then he informed us that the church executive committee was having a welcome dinner for us *sau gio* (at six o'clock). We were so pleased. At the end of the service, we greeted everyone, went home, took our siesta, and at six o'clock went back to church.

When we arrived, Pastor Chau sat, looking quite sad, and wearing his "house clothes." "Where were you?" he asked. "What do you mean?" "Where were you for your welcome dinner?" "Our welcome dinner . . . that is why we are here now." "Why are you here now?" "Well," we continued, "You said six o'clock." Puzzled look. "No, I said *sau gio nhom*" (after church). He went on to say "We had your welcome dinner and didn't know why you did not come." When we all realized the terrible language error we had made on day one, hearing *sau* (rising tone) *gio* instead of *sao* (level tone) *gio nhom,*, we had to laugh, even if we felt like crying. We had made our grand entry, missed our welcome, but were totally forgiven as we would be many more times after that.

CHAPTER FOUR

Quảng Ngãi Church

Người sẽ sanh một trai, người khá đặt tên là Jêsus. MAT 1:21

Christmas Choir

MỪNG CHÚA GIÁNG SANH
TIN-LÀNH

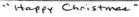

"Happy Christmas"

Pastor Châu

Quảng Ngãi
house
and
transportation

CHAPTER FIVE

MRS. CHAU

One woman had an immeasurable influence on my life in Quang Ngai—Mrs. Chau, the pastor's wife. She was a wonderful wife, mother, cook, counselor, hostess, Bible teacher, organizer, and even friend, although I never dreamed of that when I first met her. Mrs. Pastor, *Ba Muc Su* as everyone called her, was middle-aged, quiet, unschooled, and happiest when working in her backyard garden. She had one eye which did not "track" which made it difficult to know if she was talking to me. They lived in the parsonage next to the church and she could almost always be found there in her *house clothes* – silk pajama trousers and a white blouse.

Woody and I got our mail at the church mailbox located at their house, so one or both of us stopped by nearly every day. Young people always "hung out" there and often asked us about the English vocabulary they would see in our mail. Several years passed before we found out that their own three children were adopted. We especially loved Hong, the youngest, who experienced a miraculous healing from polio while we were there and who became a constant companion for our little son after he was born.

Mrs. Chau often invited us for a meal with the family. We also hosted them and the other five pastors and their wives each month to discuss the state of the Gospel in the province and what we all planned to do about it. All of us together were a true ministry team and much of our wide acceptance in the province came from the obvious love, care, and "promotion" of us by these colleagues in ministry.

One day early in our Quang Ngai experience, Mrs. Chau informed me that she wanted me to accompany her as she "went visiting" on Friday. She told me to be at her house by 9:00 a.m.and to be prepared to be away all day. I should wear my Vietnamese cone-shaped hat (called a *non*) to protect me from the sun as we would be walking a lot. Little did I know that this day would drastically change my life and ministry.

Over the next year we would go on our weekly Friday visits all over the province. These weekly visits gave me a deep love and understanding of country women and their hopes and dreams, as well as a deep appreciation for how God's Word could meet and give hope in every situation no matter how complicated or impossible it seemed. I did not know it then but I would later have wide ministry opportunities speaking to Vietnamese women within the country, as well as in the United States, which would be based on those wonderful hot and intimate Fridays in the war-ravaged province of Quang Ngai with my mentor, Mrs. Chau.

A typical day would go like this: I would bicycle down to the parsonage by 9:00, leave my bike in back, and walk with Mrs. Chau to the *"Lambro"* station a few blocks away in town on the edge of the market. This was the gathering place for vehicles that would take passengers back out into the countryside. A *"Lambro"* was basically a Lambretta motor scooter pulling a metal cart which had a narrow bench along each side for passengers. The metal sides had cut-out windows and the top had a metal roof with space for luggage (or poultry, or even sometimes a passenger) . It would take as many as ten passengers with their market goods or baggage strapped on top . . . or six comfortably. In these cramped quarters one's knees knocked the knees of the passengers across from you. You needed to find a Lambro going in your direction, bargain for a price, and get on from the back. I rode these contraptions all over three provinces and I was always a big object of curiosity as most foreigners used other transport options. I took up two seats (which I paid for).

When we got to the station, Mrs. Chau would decide which direction we would go—I guess by prayer or a nudge from God—because she never planned in advance. We would get on and she would explain to fellow passengers what we were doing. When she felt ready to visit somewhere, she would knock on the roof (the signal to stop) and we would get off. We would go to the side of the road, cross the drainage ditch and start down a dirt path or rice paddy dike. Sometimes we would be headed to the home of a believer or person from the church, but more often it would be a perfectly unfamiliar hamlet or farmhouse. The people would see us walking across the fields and they would begin to gather at the house in the direction we headed, coming from their work to check out the unfamiliar scene of midday visitors which included a big, non-Asian female.

When we arrived, they always graciously invited us inside the large thatched-roof farmhouse. Typically, these houses had dirt floors hardened like cement and swept spotless. Four huge round wood posts with hand-carved lintels way up at the top on three sides marked the center of the room; the side toward the door was open. Although there were no walls, these posts marked the center space where guests would be seated at a wooden coffee table with four chairs. The shadowy corners hid the beds; wooden platforms with sleeping mats rolled at the bottom, and down pillows with hand-embroidered pillowcases on them. The kitchen and "bathroom" were outside in the back.

We would immediately be seated around the center coffee table where a teapot and four cups or glasses on a tray permanently awaited guests. Lots of neighbor women and children crowded inside while the men stayed on the porch, unlike most events when the men were seated as guests and the women waited in the outdoor kitchen. Immediately someone from the household brought tea and we went through the formality of drinking together and being welcomed. Mrs. Chau would then begin in one of two ways. If in the home of a believing church member's house, she would ask them how they were and if they had prayer needs. She would lovingly scold them if they had not been in church and they would all promise to be there next Sunday. One time I saw her looking sternly at a "girly" calendar on the mud-brick wall . . . the only ornament in the house . . . and then stand and remove it, gently telling them it was not appropriate for a family that honored Jesus to have this in their home. Their reaction? They thanked her profusely and asked for any other teaching or training she could give them!

If it was not a Christian home, she would say "Has anyone here heard the Good News?" When asked what news she was referring to, she would sweetly say, "The Good News is that any man or woman can have a relationship with God through His Son Jesus Christ . . . ." From that she had an eager listening audience as she explained the Scripture to them. I rarely said a word; just listened, and oh, how I learned.

And then noontime came. The hostess would insist we stay for the noon meal. I never knew how this was determined, but she selected a few to eat inside with us and the rest sat outside where they could hear. The food was brought in and almost always was the same, and always wonderful. It consisted of four main items. First, there was cooked rice, unprocessed and full of B vitamins. Next, *rau muong,* a spinach-like vegetable that grows in water. Next, *banh trang nuong* which I have only seen in the Vietnamese country-side—big thin rice-paper rounds the size of a plate that had been held over a charcoal fire and "toasted" until bubbles formed in them and they were browned. All of this was accompanied by the ubiquitous fish sauce called *nuoc mam*.

The hostess would be apologetic and embarrassed to serve guests such a simple meal and not have meat or fish since they had not known we were coming, but we loved it and it made me feel like family. Much later when I taught public health in villages, I had a hard time convincing the country people that their simple menu actually held all the necessary food groups. Furthermore, the Americans discovered that *nuoc mam* is almost a perfect food with all the vitamins and minerals necessary for good health. Even though they found many hungry Vietnamese, very few were nutritionally deprived due to this fermented fish-salt brine concoction. Amazingly, without dairy products native to Vietnam, the leeched fish bones provided all the calcium they needed. This highly odorous product is used in all Vietnamese cooking and as a sauce for dipping; you will find it in our cupboard to this day. Once you get it past your nose, you are okay, and our language teachers warned us from the beginning that we would never speak Vietnamese unless we used it.

After lunch it would be time for the noon rest, so all the women dispersed to lie down on the beds . . . they simply rolled out the decorative woven reed mats and we piled on like a slumber party. The men and children hung around outside under the trees on chairs, stools, or hammocks. Some just squatted back on their heels with their hands folded across their chests and rested. All Vietnamese seem to be able to do this for hours, but my timed limit was about five minutes. No one really slept during the noon rest; the women took their cone-shaped hats to fan themselves as they talked and this was Mrs. Chau's hour to shine. There was only one problem; as an honored guest, I was not allowed to fan myself. A small boy about eight years old would be conscripted to come and get my hat and fan me for the duration. I felt silly and humbled (and always hoped no western person would see me), but was fully aware of their care and respect for me as a guest.

Quang Ngai was known for its "country accent" and I was proud I could understand it, even though the Vietnamese in the cities like Saigon always called it *que qua* (maybe equivalent of our U.S. "country hick"). In fact, the U.S. military sent linguistic experts to our place to tape me having conversations with our house helper, because the American military men who studied Vietnamese in the U.S. were learning the northern precise language and had a hard time hearing and understanding the country people where most of the bases were located.

So, week after week, I would lie on the bed absorbing the animated conversation swirling around me. I was most impressed because no matter what subject was brought up, Mrs. Chau gave good practical AND Scriptural advice. She would pull out her worn Vietnamese Bible and find just the right verse for the situation. She might have lacked "schooling," but she more than made up for it with her learning from life experience and God's Word. Once again, I saw the trans-cultural words of the Bible being skillfully applied with love and concern.

The strangest situation I remember clearly was when the hostess at one of the homes jumped up from the bed, pushed aside her coffee table, pressed something in the ground, and a huge door opened in the dirt floor. It revealed dirt steps down into a tunnel under the ground. "What should I do?" she asked the pastor's wife. "I have a son who works by day and loves our country; he is always home by late afternoon and sleeps at night. My other son comes out of this tunnel at night and fights with the Viet Cong and their co-conspirators to follow the Communist doctrine. I love both my sons and they love each other, but we are a divided house." I do not remember the answer Mrs. Chau gave, but I know this demonstrated to me how war was not only tearing apart the country, but also individual families, and how the Bible even had something to say about that.

In those days, almost all marriages were arranged. *Matchmaker* was a valid occupation and in the non-Christian homes it involved a lot of dependence on complementary signs (the Vietnamese follow the twelve animal year zodiac) and auspicious dates and other auguries. In the Christian community, the pastor's wife often played the role of free matchmaker, and I heard many a bridal gift (dowry) being discussed. Usually the young man and young woman had successfully made eye contact and figured out they were interested in one another and hinted at this obliquely to their parents. Young men and women were not allowed to communicate with each other, be alone together, or have any physical contact. Somehow it worked. The matchmaker would approach the parents and discuss the proper gold jewelry, fruit, and other necessary gifts; then they announced the engagement party. The engagement, in fact, became binding—they were husband and wife in all but sleeping together, which took place after the wedding.

Although this system has changed greatly in modern Vietnam, a lot of wisdom can be gleaned from the advice of those who love you; we saw many strong marriages growing under this system. I have tried it for many years for our son who is still happily single, but I guess I missed some element of that training.

At about two-thirty, we would get up, use the "facilities," wash up by the well, and sit again in the center of the room for tea and refreshment—perhaps a banana or mango. By four o'clock we would leave, wend our way across the irrigation dikes of the rice paddies to the road and catch a passing Lambro back to town. There I would get the mail, say goodbye to Mrs. Pastor, get on my bicycle and ride home, exhausted yet remarkably refreshed by my day out "with the girls."

CHAPTER FIVE

Pastor and Mrs. Lê Châu

Typical Country Homes

Typical
Country
Scenes

bánh tráng

Bridge
on
Route One

CHAPTER SIX

OTHER PLAYERS

Pastor Chau had warned us that the war was bad in Quang
Ngai province. As we lived there, the situation deteriorated. A small American contingent lived on a base about
two miles from us; if you followed the road from the airport
into town you would pass our house, the military hospital
across the street, the civilian hospital next to us, and then the
large prison. A bit further down was the radio station, and on
into town past the Province headquarters stood the church,
right before the main intersection. A little further down was
a shopping area and then the U.S. base at the far end of our
road. This base functioned as an advisory and "listening"
post for the Vietnamese II Division headquartered next to
them.

We had a strange and wonderful relationship with the
U.S. base; at the beginning everyone knew us, seeing we
were the only "non-governmental" civilians in town. If we
needed to go anywhere, we "hitched a ride" on U.S. military aircraft. They invited us to eat at the base whenever we
wanted to, which we often did on Sunday noon after church.
Sometimes the colonel in charge would send his driver down
to our house with special food they had gotten, or to give
notice of a particularly "suitable" movie for the missionary

family to come watch. Woody played handball with the guys for exercise and he and his partner often "won the ladder." Each day an Air America plane would come to our airstrip from Danang, and Fred, the dispatcher, would give a copy of the daily *Stars and Stripes* newspaper to one of the passengers. He would tell him to drop it off at the house next to the hospital on his way into town, so we had a different "delivery person" each day. We got up-to-date U.S. sports and event news in this remote province, and sometimes even read about our own area in the war section.

Because of the dangerous conditions, we could not go out of town in any direction, or even to the airport, before the mine sweepers would check the roads with their "carpet-sweeper- looking" devices. Often the VC would plant pressure mines under the roads at night hoping to catch a military vehicle as the first to cross an area. Almost all the time, sadly, civilian traffic such as buses bringing people to market took the brunt of casualties. Our pastors notified us when it was safe to visit their areas, especially if they wanted us to come for an evening and stay overnight. We never could stay more than one night in any place, or follow a predictable schedule, because word might get out that unknown Americans were staying in the area.

The Vietnamese military asked that we put heavy wooden shutters on the outside of all our doors and windows that could be pulled together and barred at night in case of a ground attack. The U.S. base gave us a "walkie-talkie" so we could check in each Monday evening to be sure we were okay. The problem was, we could only get good reception in the bathroom. So each week Woody perched on the toilet seat and called in "Hotspot 1-3" to report our condition. We felt loved and cared for and were thankful we could talk regularly to someone who felt some responsibility for us.

Our interaction with the military was just peripheral to our real reason for living in Quang Ngai, but it brightened many of our days, and I think theirs as well. Often when they would go on R&R, they would bring back gifts for us and especially for our son when he was born. We started a Sunday night Bible Study in English and served a light supper and dessert. Many joined us for the study, but probably as much for the tiny island of normality they felt in our home with our family. A chaplain friend took a helicopter out to get us a Christmas tree one year—it was a straggly Australian pine from a distant beach. But when we heard that they had to put an armed "perimeter" around him while he chopped it down, it became the most precious tree we had ever seen.

Within a short time more American civilians began coming to our province. Because of the number of "Internally Displaced Peoples" (IDPs) or people who are refugees in their own country, many organizations sent wonderful help. The International Red Cross set up a permanent station in Quang Ngai to deal with the continuing crisis. World Vision, World Relief, and Christian Children's Fund worked through us to help with emergency needs and sustainable development, as well as the distribution of emergency funds. The Mennonite Central Committee sent young people doing "alternate service;" this meant they were exempt from military service due to religious beliefs but were very willing to be in Vietnam for humanitarian purposes.

The American military brought over civilians to work on improvements for the civilian hospital next door to us in a wonderful program called, "Military Province Hospital Assistance Program." For a long time we never understood why the Vietnamese insisted on thinking these were French personnel. One day it dawned on us: the acronym for this organization was MilPHAP, and *Phap* is the Vietnamese word for French, so they translated it to read "French military." But they did great work! Nurse Randy, for example, completely set up and worked in the first recovery room in the country for post-surgical patients. She and I became close friends and shared a real love for the Vietnamese women.

The U.S. military assigned some medical personnel to the campaign to "win the hearts and minds of the people," and they trained young men and women in public health to go out into remote areas and provide free health care and teaching. One time an American doctor from the base came and asked me to help do this training since I was a nurse and could also speak Vietnamese. I gladly agreed to help with these classes, especially since I was provided with excellent materials and the doctor was very organized; we completed many weeks of successful training. Some time later I found out that the person who asked me was completely bogus—one of those legendary people who talked himself into a position and had all the right (but fake) papers to parlay himself into a high military medical position without being either military or medical! But I still felt good about the results and the new friends I had made.

The American Friends' Service Committee, a Quaker organization, sent personnel to build a rehabilitation ward (at the province hospital compound next door) for Vietnamese who had lost limbs. The Stickneys, a wonderful older couple, came first to set up, finance, and build the ward in a remarkably short time. Then Joe, an Englishman, came and taught the Vietnamese to make prostheses (artificial limbs) from local materials. They started with tree trunks and tanned leather and made beautiful, light, articulated limbs that functioned effectively, and became much sought after.

The war produced many amputations; so many, in fact, that technicians without any medical training performed many of them and they did a good job. At one point, an American doctor wanted to show these technicians a new method for amputating a limb and putting the prosthesis on immediately; this meant a different way to prepare the flap and stump. The new method meant that the patient did not have to learn to re-balance, and it allowed for much faster healing. They recruited me to translate and the doctor gave me the basic anatomical picture, so I could prepare my interpretation.

The doctor came down from Danang to Quang Ngai once a week, so on the appointed day for the new procedure he showed up and we went to the selected patient's bed in the ward to bring him to surgery. The patient and the nurses were all excited because he was to be the showcase, so they had given him the breakfast of his choice which he had just finished eating. "What?" The American doctor was horrified. "They fed him? We cannot give anesthesia if he has eaten." The nurses were perplexed . . . they did not understand why food would bother anyone having surgery on his leg. The doctor refused to operate and flew back to Danang.

We arranged to try again a few Thursdays later. We made it to the operating room, exposed the area for operation, started the anesthesia, and then the doctor pointed to a strange growth in the groin and asked, "What is that?" I was peering over to see when one of the technicians watching said, "Oh, that is just a *bubo*." Patient Number Two had the bubonic plague! He got sent back to bed and the frustrated doctor headed for the airstrip again. On attempt Number Three, the patient was ready but when he saw the huge group of people coming to watch his amputation, he refused to let anyone near him and actually fled on his one good leg. Soon after this the doctor's tour of duty finished so we never accomplished the goal. It is probably safe now to confess I am glad the surgery never happened because I was really nervous about the translation; most of the medical terms had no good counter-word and I was going to be pointing at "this thing" and "that thing" a lot. Those technicians might have been a very confused group.

I can't begin to name all the characters that showed up in Quang Ngai for a day or week or longer. We got lots of newspaper reporters because one could see the war "up close and personal" in our province. In fact, a certain well-known swimming hole at the river became a point of contact where a reporter could be "captured" by the Viet Cong. While swimming, he would be taken away for three days to some Viet Cong staging area in the province and given great propaganda about the righteousness of the VC cause, then sent back alive and well with three gifts. The gifts consisted of a comb made from a napalm canister, a pair of "Ho Chi Minh sandals" made from rubber tires, and a vase made from an expended brass shell casing, all of which I could buy at the local market. At any rate, the guy would come back with a great story, and usually a "new believer" just as they hoped.

Some days we would hear from a neighbor that a husband or older son was "away" for awhile. One day a teacher's wife who lived behind us told us her husband, Mai, was gone and she was not sure when he would be back. We later learned that the Viet Cong often came and abducted prominent people from an area; they would take them to their staging area and "brainwash" them for days about the Communist cause. When they were convinced, or said they were, they were allowed to return home to their normal occupation. Our teacher neighbor Mai was held for four weeks. When he came back he told us about his experience and then said, "I would have believed all the terrible things they told me about Americans if I didn't know you."

That was a sobering thought.

People came to our province from everywhere. A Dutch doctor worked for the Canadian TB hospital; a doctor from Spain spent time working with civilians; even Ted Kennedy came to see the plight of refugees, and the province advisors invited Woody to the big lunch given for him. To our shock they sat Woody next to Mr. K and asked him to serve as interpreter. He brought home a picture to prove it. In fact, at the end of the meal Teddy was trying to light his cheroot but no one seemed to have a match; Woody whipped out his lighter (a recent gift from the Korean Blue Dragon Brigade, also in Quang Ngai province) and solved the problem. I am sure that event won't be in Mr. Kennedy's biography, but it sure became a "claim to fame" for us!

For a while we even had a "hippie" trying to find himself who came and lived in our white house hostel out back; our little town was a stepping stone to a great positive change in his life, I later learned. Yes, I even knew the Vietnamese girls who "worked" at the *Green Door*, the house-of-ill-repute in town, but stopped short of visiting them "at home" to avoid any local residents from misinterpreting my mission.

Truly, in many ways Quang Ngai was like the Wild West in those days—all types of people for a great variety of reasons came and went for their own purposes—and we were in the middle of it all. There were several groups of miscellaneous, mystery Americans whose presence we knew not to ask about. All these "types" were looking for houses and helpers and translators and honest workers. We became more or less the local employment and real estate agents since we had so many contacts and could also speak the language. After these local workers received their first paycheck from their new employer they would come to our home with bananas or peanut sesame candy to thank us for getting them their job, as was their custom. We would have a wonderful visit with them that usually turned into an awesome intelligence gathering event where we found out the real facts about the employers. It would have been the envy of the professionals, if they only knew.

One American government worker fell in love with a Vietnamese girl and wanted to marry her. Her government would not give the permission for the obligatory civil ceremony, so the guy tried to get Woody to go out on a helicopter to "international waters" and perform the ceremony. He said he would have made it worth our while, but of course, Woody refused. Losing all our good faith and credibility with the Vietnamese, let alone our own standards, would hardly have been worth our while. Plus the fact that we heard a rumor that she was secretly married to a local man already.

With all of these people coming to our town, you can imagine that our Bible Study grew! We had some very exciting discussions as reporters, *peaceniks*, military officers, non-coms, and missionaries were all in the same room in civvies; none of us quite knowing the level of belief of the one next to us. We were a microcosm of the United States in those turbulent days. Most of the time we limited our study to the Sermon on the Mount because that was the only part everyone agreed was Scripture; nonetheless there was plenty in there to live by and learn from.

Woody was on the executive committee of the mission and several times a year went to Saigon for about a week. I took one of these opportunities to have my missionary friend, Carrol Henry, come and stay with me. The very day Woody left, a jeep pulled up at our house and a Korean soldier brought an invitation to our door. The Koreans were fighting alongside the U.S. and South Vietnamese troops. The invitation was for Rev. and Mrs. Stemple to come to an event the next morning at the Blue Dragon Brigade HQ about 30 kilometers north of Quang Ngai. I told the young soldier that Rev. Stemple had gone to Saigon so we could not come. "Well," he said, "this is from the general and I cannot reply with a "no," so who is this lady? Can she come? I will come and get you." So we said OK and he wrote down, Mrs. Stemple and Mrs. Henry accept the invitation.

The next day the soldier arrived. He drove us to the Brigade HQ and as we drove in we saw hundreds of Korean, Vietnamese and American soldiers assembled. A waiting soldier escorted us to a reviewing stand with five chairs on it for the American General, the Vietnamese General, the Korean General, Mrs. Stemple and Mrs. Henry. We stood as the program began. It was a presentation of medals to Korean individuals and units and it took a LONG time. TV cameras recorded it all and Carrol said, "Everyone in Seoul is probably wondering who those two floozies are standing there!" Finally, as the program ended, they led us to a long table full of hors d'oeuvres. As a combo band played and people mingled, Carrol said to me, "I hope they don't start to dance; there are only two of us here." Then gifts were presented: Carrol and I each got them as well. I remember a Parker pen and pencil set and a cigarette lighter with a blue dragon on it, among other things.

Just as we thought things were over, we were invited to go into the general's mess for a dinner. We went into a big, plain, metal building but it was beautifully decorated on the inside. It had a huge T-shaped table with white starched tablecloth, napkins, and place settings with blue dragons emblazoned on them. At the top of the "T" sat the U.S. General, the VN General, the Korean General and Mrs. Stemple, and way down the "T" with the other officers, Mrs. Henry. We still had no idea why we were invited to this big celebration, but we certainly enjoyed a multiple course meal served elegantly, plus lots of glasses filled with mysterious liquids for the toasting. I sat by the Korean general who did not speak English, so I spent much of the meal rolling my eyes at Carrol, and wondering if Woody would ever believe this.

At the end of the meal, the Korean general called for an interpreter and through him said to me, "You probably wondered why I invited you here." "Yes!" I said. He answered, "When I was a small boy in Korea, an American missionary led me to faith in Jesus Christ, and I never had a chance to thank her. Everywhere I go I look for the missionaries to honor them in her honor."

I have never felt so humbled. One single woman heard Jesus speak, responded to His call, and faithfully went to Korea under God's leading. She spent time and gifts teaching a small boy and never knew that God would use him to be a righteous leader in his nation. I couldn't wait till Woody got home and I could tell him the awesome story. And I gave him the cigarette lighter. This was the famed lighter that lit the cheroot of Teddy Kennedy; another photo that did not make the cover of our mission magazine.

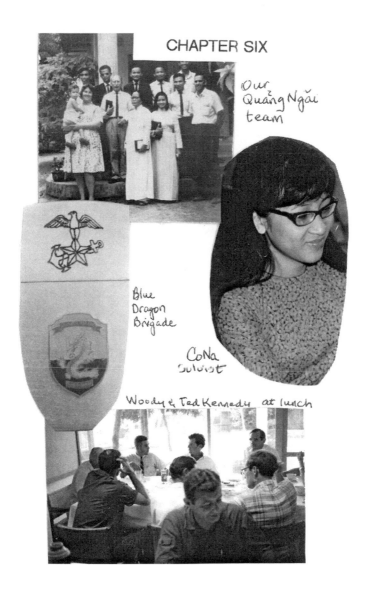

CHAPTER SIX

Our Quảng Ngãi team

Blue Dragon Brigade

CoNa Soloist

Woody & Ted Kennedy at lunch

CHAPTER SEVEN

CO THOI

When we moved to Quang Ngai, a small furnished house complete with househelper awaited us. Pastor Chau introduced us to Co Thoi telling us she was a good Christian girl from his church. Her affordable monthly wages also included her room, so she immediately moved in to the small room in our "garage" just down two steps from our kitchen door. Co (Miss) Thoi was about my age and completely different from Chi Muoi in Danang. From day one she took over our household. She did the marketing, cooked, cleaned, and did yard work — all the while talking to whoever was in earshot. She corrected our Vietnamese and interrupted when we had guests to tell them what we were really saying. She always had water boiling for the filter, rice in the pot, tea and local "peanut brittle" ready at a moment's notice for guests. She kept her ear out for the latest happenings in the neighborhood and reported to us within minutes. She held court for the neighbors out by the well, telling them everything about our life and schedule. One day someone at church asked me if it was true that I had TEN dresses? Apparently nothing was sacred; I didn't even want to think what else might be common knowledge.

She did a great job washing with our gasoline-run wringer washer, which we pulled out from the storeroom and hitched up near the well on washdays. Because of the heat and dust in Vietnam, and our constant perspiration, we changed clothes two or three times a day, so there was always wash to be done. How wonderful to have my washing and ironing so efficiently done. This reminds me that most of the time she ironed with a flat iron heated within by charcoal briquettes.

In deference to the customs of the Vietnamese at the time, I always wore skirts or cotton dresses and my sleeves always touched my elbows if not longer; they wore sleeves to the wrist. I developed a kind of culottes dress with skirt flap in front and back that was most practical and I had several made there. Vietnamese seamstresses and tailors have the deft talent of looking at a picture of a piece of clothing (or a composite such as a collar from this picture, a sleeve from another photo, etc.), measuring you, and then making a dress, suit or shirt overnight. In Quang Ngai they did it very cheaply and with a treadle machine.

As for my washing machine, Woody later found a good electric motor in the storeroom to replace the broken gas motor and he wired it on. Co Thoi was so excited. When she began to fill the tub and add the clothes, she put her hand in the water and ZAP; she almost went to heaven. Woody had forgotten to ground the 220 current. No problem; after that she would pull out the washer and literally stick the wire from the motor into the ground by the well. When the electricity was off—no problem—she went back to washing by hand again, which they really did best.

One day we came home to find a very tall bamboo pole implanted in the middle of our parking spot in the driveway. It must have been 30 feet tall and had wires connecting it to Co Thoi's room. Stuck just inside the gate, Woody got out of the van and called to her to come out and explain this strange addition and to remove it so he could get his car inside the yard. She told us she could not get good reception to her Christian radio station (Far Eastern Broadcasting Company in the Philippines) without the antenna which only worked in that spot. He told her to move the antenna so he could park the van. She insisted that surely he would not deny her that small pleasure for her spiritual growth. In his best Vietnamese, conscious we had not learned vocabulary for this exact situation, he said, "I am in charge here, and you cannot plant anything on this property without my permission. Remove the antenna." Then we went into the house and peeked out the window as she loudly complained while taking down and moving her antenna back by the well. The incident was over and we were back to normal life.

About two weeks later we were having supper and Co Thoi brought some delicious "King's bananas" to the table. Vietnam has over thirty main types of bananas and the "king's bananas" are a particularly small and delicious type that we loved. When Woody commented on the bananas, she said sweetly, "I just got them off your tree. I planted it in your yard without your permission!" She always had the last word.

When I went to teach children, Co Thoi went along—or technically, I went with her. At one point we bicycled all over the province to refugee camps and hamlets teaching about a thousand children a week. As we rode down the city streets and country roads, she kept up a running commentary on who lived in the houses, which ones were church people, what officials were good and which ones corrupt, and where to buy the best of this or that in stores or the market. Our destinations varied each time—sometimes we went to a refugee village, sometimes a schoolyard, perhaps a church, or even a vacant field in a village. She would round up the kids and get them seated on benches, on the ground or on tarps, making sure an older sibling kept the younger ones quiet. The people were always waiting for me and had my one requirement ready—a wooden table for my materials. Usually they stood around the edge of the "class" and probably learned as much as the children did. I would pop open my portable flannelgraph, attach the legs, put it on the table, and begin.

Before we went to Vietnam, a church in Pennsylvania had asked if there was something special they could get to help us in our ministry. Anticipating teaching children, I had asked for "flannelgraph materials" and they had gone overboard in supplying me. This was a commonly used Bible story teaching method where cutout figures backed with flannel are placed on a flannel-covered "board" on an easel. Different backgrounds to illustrate the story are layered on the board as the scenes unfold. I think they had gotten me every story in the Bible from Adam and Eve to the return of Jesus in Revelation, had cut out the figures and had labeled them in plastic bags. They had artistically drawn about twenty possible scenes on squares of flannel; there was no Bible story I did not have a "background" for, from the Sea of Galilee, to a palace, to a lion's den.

The portable "board," which opened like a pop-up umbrella, sprung up taut and flat ready for use. It fit into a handy long carrying case, so I felt very well equipped. In fact, while still in language study, I had the opportunity to visit some churches in Danang to teach children. At that time I still had to use a translator, so my teacher and I practiced together and, on one special occasion, went to the Lambro station and waited for one to take us to our destination. All of a sudden I saw the small crowd in the station area pointing at me, whispering and saying, *"Ba My mang sung"* – That American lady is carrying a gun. They were looking at my long wonderful folding flannelgraph equipment. "No, no," I said, "it is not a gun." I whipped it out of its case, pushed the button and SNAP, up came the flannel square. By now they were all ducking and yelling, but we had a happy ending as they realized it was NOT a gun. I showed them how it worked and what it was for; we had an impromptu Bible lesson in a Lambro station. From that time on, one particular Lambro driver would not let me pay a fare; he said he was honored to have me in his vehicle as I went to teach the children of Vietnam.

My materials worked wonderfully in a small group classroom setting, but when it came to those refugee camps or hamlets with literally hundreds of children, it typically bordered on disaster. For one thing, they could not see the figures clearly from very far back in the crowd; then the figures I had were all decked out in western clothes and they did not know why some looked like they did or dressed like they were. The lovely backgrounds stood in such stark contrast from their life experience that they were enthralled at all the "rich people." In addition, we were outdoors, so the afternoon breeze would blow the figures off which caused a huge melee as they all wanted to pick it up, feel it, check it out, and keep it. I, myself, was enough of an oddity without adding the flannelgraph method, so that experiment ended after a short trial and we taught simply by using the oral storytelling method. Also, since the Bible speaks for itself, we gave memory verses each week. The children were used to rote learning, so this became my new and improved method.

Once when Co Thoi and I were biking to a refugee hamlet about three miles south of town off Route One, we saw a huge military convoy ahead of us. There were at least one hundred U.S. military trucks parked alongside the road. Very little traffic came along, and that was just an occasional bicycle, moped or Lambro; or, perhaps some people walking with a cow or herding a few ducks along. It was a hot late morning and we had no choice but to bicycle past these trucks to get to our village. Each truck had a driver languidly standing down outside his truck smoking or talking to some children or otherwise unengaged. As we began to bicycle by, one of the drivers noticed that it was a western woman under one of those two hats. He began to holler, "Round-eye, Round-eye," and then the other drivers joined the attempt to get my attention. "Frenchy" "bonjour" and "Comment allez-vous" were a few of the nicer things they called, assuming I was French. We pedaled faster, finally got past them all and a mile down the road turned off into our dirt path back to the village where we had our class.

We not only had class in that village, we visited in the homes and enjoyed time with the families, many of whom attended the small church that had just begun there. At about four o'clock, we realized we needed to get back to town as this was one of the places the people themselves told us it was not safe to be after that hour. As we came back to the main highway, we were shocked. There was the convoy ahead of us and still parked alongside the road. Oh no, now we directly faced them and would have to ride through the gauntlet again. I sternly talked to myself and said, "You are a grown, married woman and these are nice American boys just looking for something to do, so stop and talk to them." I told Co Thoi my plan and to stick by my side, so she did.

When I heard the first one holler something in French, I rode toward him and said, "No, I'm American." The guy was shocked which resulted in a lot of fun for us all. They asked where I was from and when I said "Ohio," they called all the Ohio drivers to come around. When we told them we were missionaries, they were even more awestruck as they had no idea American civilians were anywhere near that neighborhood. When they learned where we had been, it was almost comical. "That is hard-core VC country," they told us. In fact, the reason they were waiting in that convoy was to have tanks catch up to them and lead them through the next section of highway! And we had just biked there and back.

Co Thoi and I had lots of adventures together and I found it hard to act like her "boss"; we truly functioned like friends, or even sisters. Then one time when other missionaries were staying with us, they told us that whenever we left the house a large policeman would come and visit Co Thoi in her room . . . did we know that? Well, we knew who they meant because she had introduced us to Mr. Mam as her friend's husband who happened to be the meat inspector for the town and she would get us good cuts of meat from him (that had not passed inspection or some other method I was afraid to ask about). Our friends told us we could not let this "visiting" continue as it would look like we were giving our approval. So, we solemnly told Co Thoi that Mr. Mam could not come see her any more.

A week long drama ensued which included Mr. Mam bringing us bananas which we later found out should not have been accepted because it meant we would let him visit her although no such thing was said verbally. Also, she got sick and begged us to let him bring her medicine ostensibly sent by his wife, but we remained cruel and adamant. One night about midnight, when we had no electricity, I came out of the bedroom to get another candle and saw the large form of Mr. Mam coming through the gate on his bicycle and patting our watchdog. I called for Woody who reluctantly got dressed and went out to her room. In his best Vietnamese he insisted that Mr. Mam leave and not come back. He also told Co Thoi she had to be gone with all her belongings by ten o'clock the following morning. We watched Mr. Mam go out with his bicycle, and the next morning I answered the door to find Co Thoi standing there with a bunch of bananas. I broken-heartedly refused the bananas and let her go. No one had prepared us for this language or cultural or relational challenge. And then even the pastor feared Mr. Mam would retaliate with his police power.

Things settled down; we got a new worker but it was not the same. Co Thoi got a great job with the CIA agents in town since she knew how to do everything "American style"

. . . cooking, washing, cleaning, bug control . . . and she got three times the pay I had been giving her. Mr. Mam moved her into a little house. In a few weeks she came to see me with a bunch of bananas to thank me for getting her such a good job by firing her. I took the bananas. After much more drama including a broken leg and a broken relationship with Mr. Mam, Co Thoi repented and became a good worker in the church again. She and I picked up our friendship although by then we were leaving for home assignment.

After the fall of Vietnam in 1975, I heard that Co Thoi had returned to her country village where she had grown up. Slowly she began to get news to me; she had married a man in the church; she had children, and many years later, she had grandchildren. Our lives were on parallel tracks many miles apart. Twice when I visited Vietnam as a tourist in the nineties, she came to see me and we had lunch—pho noodle soup—together. We recalled the good days of ministry together and, like all true friends, picked up where we left off; laughing a lot, overlooking some subjects, and sharing God's grace with each other.

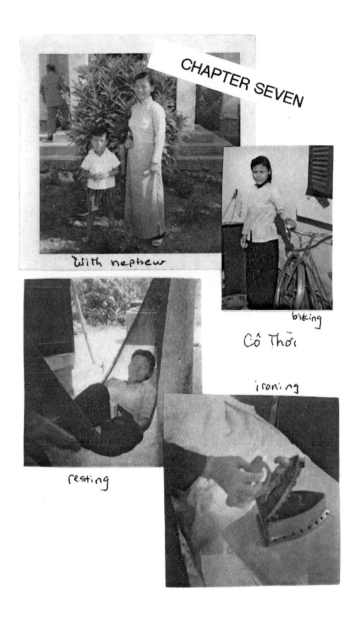

CHAPTER SEVEN

With nephew

biking

Cô Thời

ironing

resting

CHAPTER EIGHT

STEWART

We wanted so much to have children. After we moved to Quang Ngai we tried harder and drank a lot of the water. When we went to our field conference in Dalat, several of the women missionaries were talking; when they found out about my miscarriage they told me an astonishing thing. Some of them had also had miscarriages; one of them was diagnosed with a thyroid deficiency. So she self-medicated on a small daily dose of thyroid that she got from the donated medicines at our clinic. It worked for her. At least three or four others also tried it and they got pregnant. What did I have to lose? They went to the clinic, got some thyroid and told me to take it daily about three months before I wanted to get pregnant and keep it up the entire pregnancy. I went home and took the first dose and was pregnant within a month. Go ahead and scoff, but remember I am a nurse. We know this was really God's timing and in answer to many prayers of friends and family. We didn't tell anyone until three months and our "danger period" had passed; then we told everyone. Pastor and Mrs. Chau were ecstatic.

About four months into the pregnancy we flew on the weekly Air Vietnam flight to Saigon to see Doctor Tran Dinh De, the Vietnamese doctor that "all the missionaries" used (unless they had their babies in one of our clinics with our excellent, experienced nurse-midwives). When he learned we had the potential for the Rh factor incompatibility, he advised us to get monthly testing at a military hospital and if my antibody titers did not rise, to come back when I was in the 36th week (final month). He gave us a due date of May 6. We were very impressed with him, his private clinic, his modern equipment and his command of English. We flew back to Quang Ngai to show off my beginning bulge.

I went to the tailors and showed them photos of maternity clothes and proceeded to get a whole new wardrobe. Then I got my picture taken each week to mail home to the family to show my growth; sometimes standing by the bougainvillea, or under a coconut tree, or with Woody; literally dozens of expectant poses. Each month Dr Al, a Dutch-Canadian Doctor at the local TB hospital, would stop by with a vial, a tourniquet, and a syringe to take my blood. Woody would put it in his shirt pocket, go out to the airstrip and hitch a ride on the Air America chopper or anything else going to Danang, and then get another helicopter ride over to the Navy Hospital. The technicians there would test it, give Woody the verbal results, and he would fly home on the next flight he could find going back to Quang Ngai. Thank you America for your tax dollars at work! Each month we gave a sigh of relief as the blood remained normal.

We began to turn our small guest bedroom into the nursery. We had already put our sandbag bunker in that room per the request of the military for use in case of air attacks. The bunker measured about six feet long by three feet deep by five feet high. It was up against one wall and made entirely of stacked sandbags. The "doorway" was about four feet square so we had to stoop to get in. The military had also given us gas canisters for attack and gas masks for defense which we kept on top of the bunker, along with a "grease gun" they insisted we have. I had no idea how any of them worked, so was always thankful we never had to make use of them. Inside the bunker we had emergency food and water, as well as a small "emergency suitcase" filled with our important papers, passports, extra money, contact information, one change of clothes each, and some medications. We did not use the bunker much, but later it became "the playhouse" that we would all get in—once in awhile for fun and sometimes "for real."

We had a small baby bed and a dresser made by some local workers which horrified the Vietnamese. They said it was bad luck to prepare at all until the baby arrived. We didn't believe in luck but did not want to shock anyone, so stopped the preparations except for painting the room and getting some cloth diapers and generic baby things sent to us from home.

By Tet, the Vietnamese New Year, I was 7 months along, feeling and looking good. We were all set to celebrate and go visiting with Pastor and Mrs. Chau which was a highlight of our year. The first day we visited the city officials and church officers around town. The second day Mr Chau wanted us to join him in a Lambro and go visiting. "Oh no," I said, "I don't want to go on any bumpy roads or country lanes." He told me not to worry, we were just going "around here." Or so I thought. We got on that Lambro and started out to a village about 5 miles on horribly rutted cart tracks. I wanted to get out, but they kept saying we were almost there. I was mad, sad and scared I would lose my baby, but most upset that he "tricked me" to go on those roads. When I finally got the courage to confront him, guess what. He had told me exactly where we were going, but I had goofed in the language again. *Xung quanh* means around here; *Xung Quang* is the name of the village where we were headed and where we had a wonderful church and congregation. Another big laugh, apologies all around, and thankful that we had a great visit and no bad effects. Happy New Year everyone!

In mid-April we packed up and flew to Saigon. We planned to be away about six weeks, because shortly after the baby was due to be born we were to have our annual field conference in the mountain town of Dalat. We arrived at the Saigon Guest Home and settled in. How I loved that place; a big villa on a city corner in a great location, not far from central *Ben Thanh* market and an easy place to catch one of the small blue and yellow Renault taxis that were cheap and plentiful. The house had been outfitted with a big living room and dining room, as well as a manager's apartment on the first floor. Behind and above were about sixteen en-suite guest rooms that our missionaries rented at very reasonable rates. We received three wonderful meals a day, as well as tea after siesta. I always felt so pampered there. Harold and Agnes Dutton ran it almost the whole time we lived in Vietnam.

The next day we had an appointment with Dr. De. He told us things sounded and looked good and he drew some blood which he would send over to the French hospital. He then told us to come back in one week to get the results and talk over procedures. On Wednesday, April 27, 1966, we returned. I went into his office where he immediately told me my antibody titer was rising and I needed a C-section that very day; he would do it after his tennis game around 8:00 p.m. I burst into tears, ran to the door and called in Woody and repeated the message. Calmly, Woody said, "If you need a C-section, you need one; let's just trust the Lord and Dr. De." The good doctor told us to go to the Navy hospital and get some blood in case I needed a transfusion. He also told me to get some clothing, not to eat or drink anything, and come back to his clinic at 8:00 p.m. His wife would do the anesthesia. My nursing antennae were up and quivering.

So we did it. Unbelievably, we walked into the Navy Hospital in Saigon, told them what we needed, got sent to the lab where I was typed and cross-matched, and walked out into the Saigon traffic holding a bag of blood "in case I needed it." After returning to the guest home we told Agnes who called everyone in town; they all agreed to pray. That evening I checked in to my very nice private room in Dr. De's clinic while the International Church held their regular prayer service and really prayed for me. At about 8:30 p.m. Dr. De came in happy with winning his tennis match, changed his clothes, and brought me to the operating room. By now, unknown to me, my friends from church had finished prayer meeting and choir practice so they all came to the hospital and joined Woody in watching the surgery through the Operation Room window. A beautifully dressed and coiffed Mrs. De started the anesthesia.

The next thing I knew the nurses were saying in Vietnamese, "You have a boy, You have a boy." All I could say was *"Cam on Chua, cam on Bac si."* I said it so loudly over and over again that they were all laughing. It was, "Thank God and thank you Doctor." And then I groggily held him and wept with joy. Woody and all the choir members had already seen him and everyone rejoiced. All of a sudden I panicked. I began saying. *"Co muoi ngon tay khong? Co muoi ngon chon khong?"* This means, "Does he have ten fingers and toes?" I have no idea why I had this awful premonition, but I kept saying it and everyone kept reassuring me. I dimly remember foggily peeling back his blankets and counting desperately. Yes, ten fingers and toes. He weighed 7 pounds, 8 ounces and was 19 inches long and was in perfect health.

We named him Stewart David. My maiden name was Stewart and David was both a family name and the name of Woody's good friend and former roommate. The first night was awful. Woody went home around midnight and in the middle of the night Baby Stewart began to cry. He was in a crib in the room with me but I could not reach him. I had not seen a nurse since we came to the room, and I frantically pulled the bell to call one for over an hour. Suffice it to say, I did not realize that this was an upscale clinic where I was supposed to have my own nurse and an amah staying with me (or at least a husband would have done) as they never dreamed I was post-operative with no help. When we got that straightened out everything was fine.

But then I kept watching to see if Stewart would be jaundiced—the sign of an Rh incompatibility that would require a blood transfusion. No, he wasn't; yes, I think he is. All the gang came to visit me and assured me he was okay, so I finally began to enjoy him and believe that he would survive in spite of his inexperienced Mother. The doctor told me they would give me "my blood" just before discharge because we had gotten it and he didn't want to waste it. That afternoon one of my friends came in with a *Reader's Digest* article telling about unnecessary blood transfusions and how they could affect you for life, so by the time the doctor came to visit, I was in tears again. "Why are you crying?" he wanted to know. "I don't want my blood transfusion," I wailed. No problem, no blood. They discharged us after one week in good health and high spirits. We spent two more weeks at the guest house learning to parent, buying what we needed in the market, and gazing at our new bundle of joy.

We flew to Dalat on the commercial Air Vietnam flight without incident and got settled into our room with the bathroom down the hall. Because we did not know we would be having children, we felt so unprepared in many ways. I was not able to nurse completely, so we learned about formula, bottles, nipples, sterilization. We tried heating his formula in our popcorn popper, and surprisingly it actually worked. We had to buy diaper buckets since paper diapers were not on the scene, so that became a new room accessory along with soft washcloths, rubber pants, little crocheted sweaters and hats and booties for chilly Dalat. One item became totally indispensable—the pacifier. We never knew how much *WE* would become dependent on it.

Conference, as always, was wonderful. Our chairman, Grady Mangham, dedicated Stewart to God. In fact, all the children born during the past year were dedicated together; There were five of them. We took a plane back to Danang, and then an Air America helicopter down to Quang Ngai; we couldn't wait to "get home." Stewart screamed at the top of his lungs the whole forty-five minute trip, but once we landed he was happy. What a great welcome he got from the pastor and church people, as well as Co Thoi, neighbors, and just about the whole town.

I soon found out I had to live a "double life" with this baby. If the Vietnamese thought he was sleeping alone in his bedroom, they considered it akin to abuse; he needed to be with us. So when they were there we put him in our bed, otherwise in his. Because of the heat we did not always put a shirt on him—just diapers. We learned early on that putting rubber pants over the diaper in the heat would produce a rash within five minutes. When the Vietnamese saw him shirtless they would have a fit. They informed me I needed to beware of the *gio doc* (the poison wind, or what we would call a draft). And why was I saving his urine in a cloth? Their babies wore shirts with no pants; mine was wearing pants with no shirts. What to do? When in Vietnam, do what the Vietnamese do. I found out their method was actually a lot easier once you learned when and where to hold the baby out over something beside your lap.

We studied Dr. Spock's book avidly; not because we agreed with his discipline approach, but because it told us when to add items to his diet—rice cereal, gruel, mashed banana, mashed squash, eggs, bread, juices. Everything was fresh and prepared for him, no canned food. We got some childhood immunizations locally, but my sister had to send polio vaccine by mail in dry ice. He eventually got all the shots he needed—and then some—such as typhoid and cholera. We were so thankful for his good health.

In those days American babies played in playpens. So we got a catalog and showed a local man what we wanted. He really went over the top. He built a 4'x6' green bamboo playpen with a floor in it. He spaced the slats about two inches apart, and it sort of resembled a cage without a top. We kept it out by the well since it was hardly portable. Every day Stewart would get in it with all his toys, and his caregiver (a girl about 10) would climb in with him. Often the neighbor kids would climb in too. Once in awhile he even got "Dog," our scrawny watchdog, in there with him. Is it any wonder he learned Vietnamese along with English and could switch effortlessly between the two depending on who was speaking to him. His second word was *Mama*, his first was *banh mi* (bread in Vietnamese). I think *cho* (dog) came next and then *Dada*. During these wonderful days I usually sat out in the "breezeway" between our house and the garage as I studied and prepared lessons so that I could watch him and his world.

We took Stewart with us almost everywhere we went. We had tent meetings and he went; he sat with me on the women's side of church. Woody loved to carry him. So he went visiting and to market and on the back of our bicycles. He loved to ride with us on the *cyclo* — the bicycle powered conveyance with the covered seat in front. The cyclo became the transport of choice for Stewart and me as we traveled to lots of places in Quang Ngai. You had to bargain the price before you got in, and often they would give me a price break so they could "advertise." The driver would be pedaling way up high in back calling out, "Look at me, I have an American baby in my cyclo." Often they would good naturedly tell me that I should pay more since I weighed so much more than the Vietnamese. I loved it; I would tell them that when they began giving refunds to skinny women, I would pay more.

Riding down the dusty streets; waving to friends and holding our Stewart — that was life.

August 25, 1966 was our fifth anniversary. Woody was at church for a meeting and I was sitting on the front porch rocking Stewart on this beautiful night. After Woody got home rather late, we put Stewart to bed and then went to bed ourselves. Just as we were about asleep, all of a sudden the house shook as a huge explosion reverberated through the neighborhood. The blast blew out the glass windows in our living room while the shutters clanged back and forth. Woody said, "They got the big bridge downtown." I heard a commotion in our neighborhood so I tiptoed out to see what I could see. There was no electricity but I could see people running around, in and out of *OUR* gate. All of a sudden a huge military truck turned into our driveway with its headlights on our house and I could see tree limbs and debris everywhere. I ran back into the bedroom and told Woody, "Whatever it is, it is in our yard!" We both quickly pulled on clothes and ran out.

Through the melee and headlights we could see a huge crater blown in our front yard and shrapnel everywhere. The front of our house and porch were riddled with holes; it looked like measles on our walls. It seems a hand grenade had been thrown in our yard with intent to harm.

In the middle of all this, the neighbors gathered around. They all reassured us that we did not have any enemies, that they were so sorry this had happened, and that they would find out what the problem was. That was reassuring. In the end, we found out that a young neighbor girl, who lived in the squatter shacks along the road in front of our house, had mixed up her boyfriends. One of them found her with another one, so he threw a hand grenade at her and it rolled into our yard. When I saw the pockmarked front of our house the next morning and remembered that I had been sitting there with Stewart just fifteen minutes before the blast, I could only thank God again for His protection and for all the people that were praying for us. We wrote home that we had a blast on our anniversary!

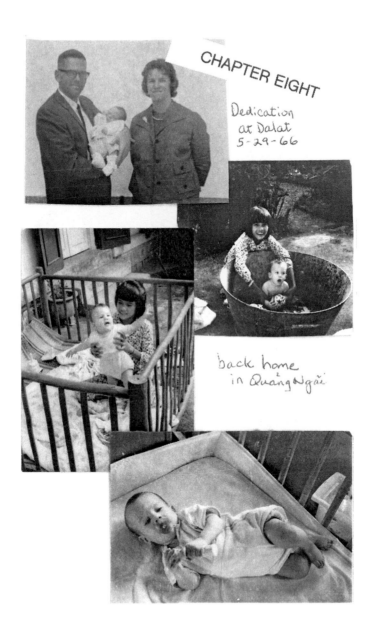

CHAPTER EIGHT

Dedication
at Dalat
5-29-66

back home
in Quảng Ngãi

Father, Son, and "DOG"

At home in Quảng Ngãi

Off to Church

L-R Sherry Herendeen
Ruth Phillips, Stewart, Lorie Frazier

one-yr.
pilot

Dalat Conference

Stewart + Jill Reimer

CHAPTER NINE

WOODY

When we moved to Quang Ngai, technically we were supposed to still be in language study. We each had a great teacher, but because we were plunged right into ministry opportunities we took our teachers along and had "on-the-job" instruction much of the time. Pastor Chau had taken us to pay a formal call on the province chief, who gave us carte blanche to travel anywhere in the province when it seemed safe. For a time, I taught his wife English and we were regularly invited to functions at their home. Each week we met with the five pastors in the province and prayed together for ways to share the good news with the people of Quang Ngai. Pastor Chau seemed happy to use Woody as his driver whenever he wanted to go somewhere for ministry purposes. Woody gained a broader understanding of Vietnamese life, language and culture on these trips around town and throughout the whole province. Pastor Chau told me repeatedly, "Woody is such a good driver!"

About a year after we arrived, the pastors decided they wanted to hold a province-wide tent meeting. They knew that a colleague of ours, who was born in Hue of missionary parents and therefore spoke the language fluently, had recently acquired a big tent in which to hold evangelistic meetings.

The date was set, the evangelist agreed to come, we secured special music, and the province chief granted permission for us to hold the meetings in the big vacant lot across from the province headquarters right downtown. We planned our advertising, and a printer in our church made nice posters to put up all over town.

However, the Vietnamese were used to getting their information a different way. In our province whenever there were special events such as malaria training, a government function, or notice of a market relocation, for example, leaflets would be dropped from planes. The health department, the *psywar* outfit, and others had small planes which would fly over at least weekly and small square printed paper leaflets would flutter like snow to the ground. People would run to get them and even collect them. We found out later that was because they were the perfect weight for toilet paper. Reading those leaflets was the main way we knew the local news.

So Woody decided he wanted to advertise our tent campaign that way. He asked some guys in the local *psywar* office to print up the leaflets, got a pilot buddy from his handball ladder to agree to push them out the back of his plane next time he had a flight, and the plan went off beautifully. As the C-123 lifted off from the local airstrip nearby, Woody called to me from the study, "I think this is our leaflet drop," so we ran outside to watch. Sure enough, advertisements fluttered all across the province and everyone got the word in plenty of time.

We found out later that our drop did cause a few mishaps. Because the drop was done quite soon after the printing, the ink did not have sufficient time to dry and some of the papers stuck together in clumps. One clump fell in a local Buddhist pagoda yard and the monks expressed their displeasure at this forceful invitation. Worse yet, two or three clumps fell on the Vietnamese military headquarters and landed on the roofs with such a loud noise they thought they were being bombed and went on "red alert." After reporting this to their U.S. counterparts, the "powers-that-be" said that any plans Woody made hereafter were to be run by the base commander first.

The week came, expectations were high; the speaker, singer and friends came and piled into our little house. A C-130 flew the tent into Quang Ngai and local church people trucked it into town and assembled it. They also built a makeshift stage and wooden benches which they put into the tent. Bare light bulbs on a maze of wires hung all around the area. The little pump organ and PA system were the last to be installed. We placed special chairs in the front row for the dignitaries who had promised to come to the opening service. We all prayed in great anticipation of the next day.

Then it began to rain. It was not rainy season—it was not monsoon season—but it was a deluge. And it did not stop. The skies were leaden, the ground was sodden, and the water inside the tent nearly rose to the level of the bench seats. Now what? The program had to go on. Woody and the speakers went there early trying to wipe off seats and keep the lights on. A few people straggled in, the dignitaries sent their regrets, and everyone sat soggy and chilled. I bundled up little Stewart and caught a cyclo which I paid to wait for me. The audience had to sit on one bench and put their feet on another.

The rain persisted for five nights. We felt discouraged, disgruntled, and doubtful. The nightly crowd was small and the response was so disappointing. When the meetings were over and the guests went home, it took another two weeks for the tent to dry off and get sent back to Saigon where it came from.

But God's plans differed from ours. A few weeks later, a strange thing happened. People began to come in to the church and ask for the pastor. They would say things like,

"Our whole village had planned to come to the tent meeting but because of the weather only I could come. I took back the message the best I could, but now the people want to hear more. Can you come?" This happened not just once, but five or six times. Some even brought petitions signed by many people asking for more news about the Good News. Within the next months Woody, the pastor and teams from church—and often Stewart and I—would go to these locations and share the Gospel message from God's Word in their language, and it took root. Teams would then go weekly and disciple the new believers who lived now with hope and joy and expectancy. We loved to hear them sing, and were blessed when they asked that we teach their children. In our eyes the tent campaign failed miserably; in God's plan it made an eternal difference.

At this time many of these people lived in refugee dwellings, or small country hamlets. Their "homes" were usually one room in a long building of many rooms. These were made from dried mud plastered over bamboo with thatched roofs. They had no place in their hamlet or refugee village large enough to have a meeting. Woody designed a simple plywood building set on cement blocks with a tin roof. Simple wooden, backless benches made by the believers would seat up to 100 people inside the building. *Tin Lanh* (Good News) was painted over the front door, and we could worship there. Many chaplains took offerings and helped buy the plywood and the tin, but the people did the work themselves and all of us gave God the glory. I think we had twelve or more of these village chapels.

Whenever Woody took Pastor Chau anywhere, Woody prepared himself to be frustrated. The Vietnamese country people functioned with "event" orientation completely opposite of a time oriented westerner. An event would begin after everyone arrived and conclude when everyone got done saying what they wanted to say. A preacher who only preached twenty minutes short-changed the congregation. Pastor Chau would always tell Woody a time to come or go to something; Woody would always be there on time but Pastor Chau was never ready. We would arrive and Pastor Chau would come to his door in his "nap" clothes—his white shirt and shorts. He would look surprised that we were there; Woody would remind him that he had told us to be there at that time. Pastor would get dressed; we would have some tea together, and then he would be ready to go. When we got to the place where a service had been announced, no one would be there. After our car arrived, people would begin to come. This was the one area in which Woody would not adapt; he held no animosity and would wait contentedly, just so he was not the one "late." Nothing in this area changed during our entire time in Vietnam. As for me, I learned to live with a lot less tension when I would just "go with the flow."

Teaching English was another of our many activities. In the first half of the twentieth century, the well educated Vietnamese learned French. When the French left in 1954 after their stunning defeat at the hands of Ho Chi Minh's forces at the battle of Dien Bien Phu, Vietnamese became the official language and English became the second language of choice. Now everyone wanted to learn English and came to our house to ask for lessons, both private and in a class. After conferring with Pastor Chau, we felt this would best fit in as a part of our working with the young people.

We opened English classes on Saturday evenings, followed by a youth gathering, which became very popular. Eventually, at the request and approval of the church, Woody raised funds for them to build a youth center and Christian education unit attached to the church to be used for Bible studies, children's classes, and especially youth gatherings. We loved the youth gatherings; they were always spontaneous and everyone got involved. At the beginning we were hesitant to take our turn at guessing an answer, singing a

song, or doing some crazy thing, but soon we were participating and I even became famous for a little ditty I learned
in their poetic style. "Refreshments" were usually bread and
a pickle mixture, fruit, non-sweetened crackers or cookies;
the Vietnamese did not crave sweets like we did. I would get
my "sweet fix" from the wonderful peanut brittle covered
with sesame seeds for which our Quang Ngai province was
famous.

The Vietnamese highly value education. All the children attended some sort of school until grade five, so the
literacy rate is over 95%. At the end of grade five they took
a comprehensive test, which meant their entire future was at
stake. Because of the small number of higher schools, those
who failed were finished with school and went into the work
force. Those who passed went to a sort of middle school for
three years. Then they took another test and went on to high
school . . . or not. At the end of grade ten a huge test was
given which allowed them to complete high school and enter
college. These tests were very competitive and very emotionally hard on the youth. Only larger towns and province
centers had high schools, so students from the countryside
who passed the tests had to move to the city and find lodging
to go to school.

Woody decided we could build a hostel in our yard to
have some of the Christian students come to live during their
school sessions. We could also mentor and disciple them.
So he got a foundation built, procured the plywood and tin,
and hammered together our backyard hostel. He painted it
totally white and the residents promptly gave it the name
"The White House." We screened in the windows, and the
military gave us cots and blankets for twelve. We opened
"The White House" for business. The students cooked and
got water by our well and used our local-style "squat pot"
bathroom in our outside building. They loved it, and so did
we. I can still hear them studying by rote in their stylistic,

out-loud manner as they memorized. A good student would be able to recite to the beat of the teacher's ruler on the desk.

Quang Ngai had five prisons within the province. The huge main prison was just down past the hospital from our house and held about 2000 civilian prisoners. The other prisons were for the military and political prisoners. *Chieu Hoi* prison was a military prison for Viet Cong who turned in their arms and came back to the government fold; they were sent to *Chieu Hoi* for re-education and then released back into society. We had become friends with the prison warden and he had told us we had permission to go into any of the prisons to teach the Good News.

The pastor, a team of youth including singers and musicians, Woody and I went to the big prison and at least one or two of the other ones weekly. The guards would bring ALL of the prisoners into a huge hall with cement floors and seat them on the floor. They would be waiting for us when we came. About fifteen of us would come in and sit on chairs in front of them, and using microphones, would hold a "church service" which included singing, humor, Bible stories with a moral lesson and a challenge to give their lives to Jesus. They listened without a whisper of sound and upon hearing an invitation, many often accepted the challenge. The pastor and team would pray with them. How exciting to see how they sensed the hope and love this new life had to offer.

After awhile so many became believers that we felt a real need for further training and teaching. The warden agreed and arranged for us to come an hour earlier, and he would have the believers there. The next week when we showed up, to our amazement he had put up a huge sheet on wires which divided the room front and back. All the prisoners were again brought in, but the believers were invited to sit in front of the sheet and the unbelievers behind it. Everyone could hear the same message because of the speaker system, but only the believers could see us teaching. Each week the sheet moved further and further back; we never knew if there were really more believers or they just wanted to sit in the front with the "good guys." Later on, we were to learn just how deeply the Gospel had taken root in the prison. I became good friends with some of the women prisoners; they often gave me hand-embroidered gifts they made while there waiting the outcome of their sentences.

Later, while visiting in the United States, I saw a morning talk show where the host was interviewing a well known celebrity about Vietnam. They discussed torture in Vietnamese prisons and to my utter astonishment they brought up the Quang Ngai prisons. They alleged horrible conditions such as wooden plank beds and beastly torture to the women. I was dumbfounded. Neither of these two had ever been to the province, let alone the prison, and I had been there weekly for months up until a few weeks before. Besides that, all Vietnamese sleep on wooden beds without mattresses. I am not naïve and some torture possibly had taken place, but with my weekly visits and good friends, I felt betrayed by the media that painted such a picture when the warden tried so hard to better the conditions. I tried very hard to talk to the people involved, but my opinion was not heard.

Woody could have had many "titles" for what he did; no two days were the same. One title could have been "labor negotiator." One day I came home from teaching to find about thirty-five Vietnamese women sitting under the mango tree in our front yard. I tried to find out what they wanted but their spokesperson said they were waiting to talk to "Mr. Missionary." They would not give me a hint which made me really curious and a bit worried by the time Woody got home. When he finally got home and figured out their problem, we had to laugh. They needed a labor negotiator and Woody happily obliged. It seems these girls all worked in the mess hall down at the base and had heard of Vietnamese workers in Danang "striking" for better pay. So they decided to try it, and they told the crusty sergeant in our town that they were going on strike for better pay. In response he told them to go ahead; then he fired them all and put out word that he was looking for new help. So, they panicked and needed a sympathetic translator, thus coming to visit Mr. Missionary. Woody went down and interceded with the sergeant for them. The day's events ended up satisfactorily; Sarge hired them all back . . . and at slightly higher wages than when he fired them, and we all "lived happily ever after."

Sometimes I called him the "universal blood donor." Because of the lack of resources, and because of the Vietnamese fear of giving blood (most did not understand replacement physiology and thought they were giving it forever), the hospital always needed blood donors. There was no such thing as a blood bank. Since we lived next door and since he was almost always willing, the Vietnamese nurses or doctors would often come over to find Woody when they needed blood. And I mean often. He would go over to the hospital, lie down on the gurney, and bare his arm. His veins are huge. In fact, I once told him that was why I fell in love with him; I could find his rope veins and start an IV in the dark.

They would put the needle in and take 200 cc of his dark red O positive blood from one arm. Then they would put the needle in the other arm and take another 200 cc. They took twice as much blood from Woody as they would from a typical Vietnamese. Then he would sit up, pull down his sleeves, and get off the table. They would *ooh* and *aah* and call him Superman, but eventually conclude he could do that because he had American blood! I have no idea how many lives he saved or pints he gave, but a lot of Quang Ngai people were walking around with U.S. blood! Woody was actually a living illustration of what he had come to teach; the Good News that the blood of the God-man Jesus could save their lives for eternity.

CHAPTER NINE

Tom Stebbins

The Tent Meeting

The "White House" hostel

The Youth Center

Teaching at the Quang Ngai prison

CHAPTER TEN

REFUGEES

Shortly after we moved to Quang Ngai, the refugee phenomenon began; the fighting in the remote seacoast and mountain areas of the province intensified so severely that thousands of displaced Vietnamese poured into the provincial center for safety. Within our first year, the population swelled; the public services were severely strained, markets were depleted, and the already substandard medical facilities floundered. Many humanitarian agencies came to help, and we assisted many of them to get connected locally. Personnel arrived to stay in Quang Ngai from the Mennonite Central Committee and American Friends Service Committee, among others.

World Vision offered to build a complete village for refugees and put Woody in charge. He was able to help the people help themselves do this. They built long buildings with individual one or two room units for families, kitchen areas behind the buildings and community "facilities" even further back. A good well stood at the center of the community and each family soon had a garden plot. The village had a school and a church from day one and became a model for other villages with their industry and desire to be self-sufficient. But still, the pain of being uprooted was evident everywhere..

As more and more refugee communities sprang up, we involved ourselves in the emergency phase as well as the long-term phase. We distributed rice, cooking oil, sleeping mats, blankets, cook stoves, and fuel oil. The item we had the most of was called bulgur wheat—I called it vulgar wheat—which we also had to teach them to use. It needed to be soaked before cooking and was best used to stretch the rice rations and not eaten by itself. It was worth the effort as it was replete with B vitamins.

Wonderful help came from all over the world. One day an aid group member came and told me a baby food company planned to donate hundreds of pallets of baby food – could I use it? The only "hitch" was that I would have to write a report of how I distributed it. I was thrilled as getting good nutrition to infants was a big need. The baby food arrived but what a disappointment—the whole shipment was made up of one flavor—strained prunes. That was the one thing we certainly did NOT need. You would not want to read the report I sent in. Other items donated to us to be given to the refugees included sweaters, clothing, and toys and playthings such as dolls, marbles, jumping jacks, jump ropes, chalk and other welcome items.

Every Vietnamese home and store whether rich or poor, large or small, ornate or plain; has an ancestral shelf, and the refugee homes were no exception. In most homes the shelf holds a picture of the parents or ancestors, a vase of flowers, some incense, and a plate of fruit which is regularly refreshed. Although considered a Buddhist nation, Vietnamese Buddhism is not a strong form of Buddhism such as is practiced in Thailand or Cambodia. Vietnamese venerate their ancestors and hold a Confucian morality or ethic.

When a Vietnamese becomes a believer in Jesus, he no longer worships or pays obeisance to his ancestors, so he removes the objects from the shelf. However, he still honors and respects them and often keeps their photos on a table nearby. Sometimes he replaces the shelf objects with a Bible and hymnal which he may read daily to his family, as well as carry to church. What a surprise to go to the village where we had given each family a doll and find that beautiful doll up on the family shelf with the rest of the revered objects!

Even if we had not given toys, the children were very creative. They made wagons with wood block wheels and pulled each other around; they played pick-up sticks with real sticks. Their jacks and a ball were pebbles and a stone, and they pushed round rocks with sticks to keep them rolling. Each village had a soccer ball which was the most prized possession. Evenings were often spent playing a form of badminton over a makeshift net with home-made rackets. Even though the uprooting was painful, the children played and ran and sang and made the most of their new situation. One day the Red Cross workers came to get me; they had gotten five truckloads of something to give to the kids and they needed me to explain these items. They were hula hoops with bells in them! Words failed me, and so did my poor demonstration, but the children caught on right away and they became very popular.

Schools were crowded even before the refugees swelled the population. Children sat so closely together that everyone was forced to be right-handed; there was no room to work with your left hand. Classes were content laden and only half day with no such thing as recess or "fluff" subjects. Teachers would send one class home at noon and come back after a brief rest to the afternoon classes. We oversaw the building of several schools in small refugee enclaves which enabled these children to experience a semblance of normalcy as they again picked up their daily routine of learning.

In the wonderfully precise way of the Vietnamese language, there are several ways to say "orphan." There is the orphan who has lost both father and mother; one who has lost just a mother, or just a father, or the father who is away in the military. Some were orphans because they were abandoned by a father who might have taken a second wife and family. During this critical time, many overseas people lovingly supported "orphans" of one description or another with monthly gifts which paid for their food, schooling, and uniforms. In the Vietnamese system, the government provided the teachers but the students had to provide uniforms, textbooks, and pens. It was wonderful for us to assist in pairing caring sponsors with these needy and worthy children.

We took Stewart everywhere, except to the refugee camps. When we took him there the people wanted to touch him and watch him and then begged us to take their children with us and raise them with Stewart. I felt that the contrast between our child and theirs was just too great; not in culture or appearance, but in any hope for a future. Working with refugees, which was to become one of the themes of my future, was the hardest thing I ever did. Every single time I entered a camp, village or compound with refugees, I was aware that I could walk back out and they could not. I had an idea of what might happen the next day or the next week; they did not. I had adequate food and clean water; they did not. I had meaningful work; they did not. I could get to medical care; they could not. I had hope, they had none. I had willingly left my home and could return there in the event of an emergency. Disaster had forced them to leave their homes and they probably could never return. My future depended on my choices; theirs depended on some official's whim. But it was in these situations that I saw the Good News take root and the reality of HOPE and LOVE make the most radical difference, so we kept going back.

Even in the most tense times, something would always happen that lightened our lives with a bit of humor. Usually it was a big cultural booboo or language error we made, or it could be a guest who came unannounced to see how we lived there. One time it was Fresca. All of a sudden, the U.S. government banned products with cyclamates since they had been found to cause cancer in rats. Therefore the military food supplies had to be examined to see if any contained this chemical. Supposedly the veterinary division oversaw food safety. At any rate, the base had a huge supply of Fresca which could no longer be made available to American military personnel because it contained cyclomates..

Instead of throwing it all out, they trucked it down to us and we piled it up in our garage from floor to ceiling; thousands of cans. We gave it out to our churches, refugee camps and villages without qualification. We also drank it ourselves . . . a lot. It occurred to us afterward that we might have had a big enough sampling to research the effects of cyclamates in humans and been more precise than the original test with rats.

About the same time a breakfast food manufacturer must have had a big over-run of the product called Pop-Tarts. I think World Vision received a whole shipload and sent them all over the country to the missionaries. In Quang Ngai we got 900,000 Pop-Tarts—I am not kidding! And no toasters. The Vietnamese loved them and so did we, but I still can't walk down the pop-tart aisle in the grocery store without a shudder. The highlight came one day as we were attending a communion service in a country church—with Pop-Tarts and Fresca as the communion elements.

Death became an everyday occurrence in the camps. Burying a loved one far from his ancestral plot devastated the already camp weary refugees. When Vietnamese die, at least in the countryside, they are not embalmed. They bring the body to the house to be cleaned and put into a plain red, wooden coffin. The family hires mourners to play local instruments and walk with them in procession to the grave — a family plot in the country, or a cemetery in the city. In the city there would be a separate cemetery for each faith. All the mourners wear white tattered garments and sometimes have dirt or ash on their faces and heads. For me, seeing a Vietnamese funeral made the Biblical accounts more real as Jesus spoke of wearing sackcloth and ashes. He also saw a funeral procession as He was walking along through the countryside.

One day a little girl came to our door while Woody was out of town. She was about eight years old and I recognized her as a bright student in one of my many refugee camp children's classes. She was sobbing as she told me her mother had just died in the province hospital next door. Her little brother came with her and the hospital had told them they had to get their mother from the hospital morgue within twenty-four hours. Their father was in the Vietnamese military stationed far away and they had no way to get news to him. They begged me to help them. I brought them in to the house, held them, wiped their tears and discovered they really wanted to take her back to their home village of Nghia Hung where we had a little country church and pastor. So I agreed.

I took my house helper along and the four of us went to the hospital warehouse in the back that served as the morgue. Rows of simple, bright red wooden boxes were stacked there waiting for family members to come and retrieve their own. The children identified their mother, and the workers put the box in the back of our VW van. I started driving into the country. The only road bumped and rattled its way through rice fields and bamboo groves. Then we came to a small stream which we had to cross on a makeshift bridge fashioned from iron railroad tracks with some half-sawn logs and bamboo trunks tied between them. It was just wide enough for our van and I would have to navigate perfectly. I did not want to go on.

But then I looked at those precious children and said a fervent prayer. My helper got out of the car and walked ahead of me on the bridge motioning me to right or left to get my car on. I have been reminded of it since when starting to go through a car wash; the difference was that there was no floor and no conveyer belt; I had to get on those tracks perfectly and then proceed on them for about 30 yards. I don't think I breathed till we reached the other side.

When we got to Nghia Hung, we delivered the body and the children to the pastor at the church. He took over from there. I was never so glad to reach a destination. The ride back frightened us just as much, especially as it was "after hours" to be in that neighborhood, but the adrenalin and prayer got us home safely. About a month later we had a knock on the door. A young Vietnamese combat soldier in full uniform stood there with a bunch of bananas in his hand and two familiar children at his side. He had come to give us thanks for the love we had shown in his hour of need. It was the least we could have done. And it made up a lot for the scolding I got from Woody for daring to drive on that road in that neighborhood at that time.

The Quang Ngai province "ambulances" passed our house many times a day en route to the hospital next door. They consisted of two men, front and back, each carrying one end of a pole on his shoulder with a hammock slung between them carrying the patient. They jogged along in cadence to get their friend or neighbor to help as quickly as possible. Nursing care consisted only of dispensing medication, monitoring IVs, and dressing wounds similar to other third-world country hospitals. Therefore the patient always needs someone there to do custodial care such as bathing, cooking, providing meals, running errands, and doing laundry for clothes and bed linens. A family member or two comes along and stays on a mat beside or at the end of the bed to help in these ways, so the wards are all quite crowded.

If the sick individual is coming to the clinic or to see the doctor at the hospital, he will probably have to wait in a long line or crowded hall where a nurse or secretary has control over the line. If a person is prominent, he or she will possibly be called into the room first. I did not know this at the beginning of our time in Quang Ngai, so I felt quite flattered that people often stopped and asked me to accompany them to the clinic next door. As we entered the crowded hall, I would sit and visit with the sick person, feeling quite noble. Almost every time, when the nurse opened the door to call the next person, she would spot me and call me in with my friend. As soon as I recognized this practice, I began to say with a smile, "No, these other people were here first, please take them first; we will wait." This solved two problems. People didn't come get me anymore and I was able to make a small dent in the accustomed unfairness of life for the rural poor and refugees. But, at least they had a hospital and access to it, with dedicated personnel who were eager to learn.

Most of the doctors who worked at the province hospital also had their own private practices so the more wealthy persons in town could go directly to their offices and avoid the clinic hassle. In fact sometimes these people, feeling tired from a trip to Saigon or a busy day, would call the doctor to their home for an IV infusion of saline solution to pep them up. They urged me to take advantage of that and did not believe me when I told them a few glasses of lemonade and some extra *nuoc mam* on my rice would take care of everything. Thankfully, we enjoyed good health most of the time and our many visits to the hospital were to help others.

Refugee Camps

CHAPTER TEN

a blown-up bridge

Refugee
Chapels

The Refugee
Committee

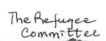

The neighbor's
Wedding

CHAPTER ELEVEN

NO TWO DAYS ALIKE

I could never describe a typical day in Quang Ngai because no two days were ever the same. Our life was challenging, dramatic, and fulfilling and we began each day praying together that God would give us what we needed for that day. The war was intense and always there. Our big activity for the day with Stewart consisted of standing by our gate to watch as the tanks rumbled past our house out to the airfield perimeter in the late afternoon and returned in mid-morning back to the base. The men in the turrets always waved at us and Stewart loved to wave back.

Woody and I often remarked how we wished that we had stock in a barbed wire company. The South Vietnamese government and the U.S. military strung up the big rolls of concertina wire everywhere. We saw it rolled around almost every civilian government building as well as each military installation. Every military gate, bridge abutment, and highway checkpoint had rolls of the wire across it which had to be moved to enter or exit. The airfield had a perimeter of the wire protecting the small runway in our town. Even the hospital was "protected" by rolls of wire and of course the prison had it as high as the walls. I always wondered who was safer—the persons inside or outside of the wire.

Sometimes the war would sound close and we three would go into the "playhouse," a.k.a. the bunker, for a while. We often got false alarms and really depended on our neighbors to keep us informed about the local situation. One evening Dave, a Peace Corps worker from Laos, was visiting us and we started playing dominos. Someone knocked on our door and Woody opened to find one of the men in U.S. military intelligence. He said he needed to talk to Woody privately. They whispered together and the man left. Right away we asked what he had said and Woody admitted he said that they had intelligence that one of the houses belonging to foreigners was going to get a satchel charge that night. He advised us to have one of us stay up and keep watch. Woody and I voted for Dave to stay up and we slept soundly. As far as we know, Dave also went to sleep and no one was a target that night.

World Vision told us they were sponsoring an evangelistic duo named the Palermo Brothers to come visit many of the mission stations in Vietnam. They would be in Quang Ngai for four days and wanted to work, and not just sit around. They were willing to minister to GIs or Vietnamese. They were guitar and accordion players and did comedy as well. At that time they were quite well known in the United States because of their ministry with Youth for Christ. They often put on huge spaghetti suppers and played on their Italian heritage to do some stand up comedy along with their music, which was primarily religious. They had written a book called *I'ma Louie, 'Atsa Phil,* which had become their signature introduction. I had seen them in my hometown of Akron, Ohio and enjoyed them, but I wondered how they would cross cultural lines. However, we took them at their word and booked them all over.

We were so excited when they arrived but almost immediately ran into our first hitch. They had electronic equipment, and the places we had booked them had no electricity.

We had been there so long we hadn't thought of that. But they adapted and were good sports to do some gigs with just the acoustic guitar and accordion; do others with generators; and really pull out all the stops at the places we had electricity. Their jokes, primarily based on their ethnicity, were impossible to translate so some dynamic equivalents were given and the people laughed in all the right places—mostly at their antics and expressive crazy faces.

Phil and Louie, for their part, loved our town but were scared to death the whole time they stayed there. After the first night in our guest room they met us at breakfast to ask if we had gotten any sleep. Assuring them we had, they could not believe we hadn't heard the shooting all night. We had become used to it and hoped it was always outgoing. They had been unable to sleep a wink and sat up and taped it, insisting on playing it back to us for most of the morning.

They had a show one night at the U.S. base and the men there loved it. The military men gave the brothers souvenir uniforms and boots which they wore the rest of their stay. Woody also took them to some smaller bases out in the surrounding areas which never got the big shows, and they were well received. At the conclusion of their concerts at the bases they would ask for favorites. Fulfilling the requests showed off their wide repertoire. At one place a soldier asked if he could borrow one of their instruments and he proceeded to play beautifully, far better than either Palermo brother. They found out he was a well-known professional in his field and they had made his week.

Phil and Louie liked it so much that they came back to Quang Ngai the next year and I can remember them writing their dramatic Christmas newsletter in our guest room. The printer in our church produced it free of charge for them. This time we had one occasion where I took them to a base which had heard a "USO show" was coming. When they saw Phil and Louie get out of our van, there was loud booing and hissing by the GIs, and calls of "Where Are the Girls?" True showmen that they were, the Palermos soon had the men eating out of their hands. I am not sure how much they accomplished for the Kingdom, but I know they brought laughter and truth to some battle-weary men and had a good time with our Vietnamese church family as well.

Woody and I took our annual trip to Saigon one year. We happily signed in and relaxed at the Guest House, happy to see our friends and anticipating a few days off. Word got out that we were there and a delegation of women from the main Saigon church came to visit me. These women went weekly to visit the women's prison in Saigon to hold a Bible teaching service. They had heard we were familiar with prison work in Quang Ngai so they came to ask me to be the speaker at their next meeting in a few days. I had heard terrible things about the Saigon women's prison; how they would do passive protesting by coughing constantly any time an official wanted to talk to them; how they were hardened and recalcitrant. I did not want to go.

After lots of persuading, I agreed to go as I had brought some lessons along with me. On the appointed day they picked me up and we arrived at the prison, a one-story structure of many wings. We had to walk through rows of cells on our way to the auditorium and the women were all sneering, staring, and smoking. They were pointing, calling out, and wondering who I was and what I was doing there. I was petrified.

Guards brought the women into a large room and seated them on the cement floor; our delegation of six was seated on chairs at the front. As the leader got up to start the meeting, I felt God prompting me to change my message and to talk about the Prodigal Son. Oh no, I had not practiced the vocabulary for that story. "Look in your Vietnamese Bible," I thought. "The story there has all the words you will need." Leafing quickly, I found the beautiful story in Luke 15 and when my turn came I got up to share it with this hardened crowd. You could have heard a pin drop. I believe God took over and told His story and showed them His picture of His wide open arms for these women. Sinners all are we, deeply loved and welcomed by the Father. I could hardly get out because of their desire to shake or touch my hand. My church women friends who returned weekly said they always had a great reception after that. It was a great faith building experience for me, but I still was glad to go home to my friends in Quang Ngai prison where I felt much more at home.

One day when the fighting was intense and the road to Danang had been cut for a long time, the town got very low on supplies such as fuel for the generators and vehicles. Some nurses came and asked if they could have some of our coconuts as the hospital needed them. Our small property was ringed with about twenty lovely coconut palms and we regularly enjoyed the "juice." To get it, someone had to climb up the tall tree (using his hands and knees to propel him upward) and cut the coconut off the branch; shinny back down and then hack off the top of the coconut with a machete. The clear liquid was ready to drink, either by a straw or from a pitcher filled with the liquid and some scoops of the fresh slimy white meat added. We loved it and there was nothing more refreshing on a hot day. We readily gave consent for them to take as many as they wanted, thinking they would drink them.

When we noticed they were very careful to cut only fresh young coconuts, we inquired about their use. To our shock, the nurses said that the hospital was out of intravenous fluids and needed the fresh coconuts to supply this. I actually saw them bung the IV apparatus into the coconut and put the sterile liquid directly into patients' veins, but in most cases they put it in a sterilized bottle and infused it the usual way. I wish I had pictures. Apparently, a young coconut has the same Ph as Ringer's Lactate and contains

500 – 800 cc of liquid. Incredible. They told us the Viet Cong or North Vietnamese always used coconuts for IVs on the Ho chi Minh trail, and I have since learned that the communists in Malaysia pioneered this in the Malayan jungles as they fought the British. The problem is that if the coconut is too old the sugar content changes and you can easily send the patient into "la-la land."

About this same time we had lost our electricity and had to suffer for days without fans during the hottest season of the year. We carefully treated our water but had no way to get it cool or make ice. We had resorted to constant hand-fanning and sweat-mopping, and we slept tossing and turning all night. One day I was lying in our breezeway in a hammock studying a lesson when I heard the call of the vendor coming down the street, *Kem sua, kem cay; kem sua, mua day.* The popsicle boy.

Don't even think U.S. popsicles; these were small fruit flavored ices less than half the size of a U.S. popsicle with a big bamboo toothpick stuck in it. A young boy had a grimy Styrofoam box-like holder slung on his shoulder with ice inside to help keep the popsicles cold until he had sold them all. "Oh, I would LOVE a popsicle, but I don't dare buy one," I thought. "I do not want to get sick from the unclean water." He called again, closer this time. I wondered if freezing destroyed germs. By the time he got to my driveway I jumped out of my hammock, throwing caution to the wind. I called to him and purchased not one, but five, mango popsicles. I stuck them in a paper cup and savored them to the last drop. The temporary cooling outweighed the chance of getting sick, which I never did.

The next Sunday at church Mrs. Am approached us and invited us to lunch at her house that day. I had not really met her but had noticed that she always wore a long string of lovely green jade beads. After church we went to their home where we had a delicious family meal and a good time with her children, especially her daughters who were key leaders in our youth group. After eating, Mrs. Am invited us to visit their "factory" located behind their house. Unknown to us, they operated a big ice plant and she carefully showed how the health department regulated and checked their water supply: their products were totally safe. Then she showed me that part of their plant was involved in making popsicles. Oh, joy! After that visit I think I became the "Popsicle Queen" of Quang Ngai. Never mind the dilapidated Styrofoam box and the even grimier hands that fished out the flavors!

The first year in Quang Ngai we were technically still in "language study" and were allocated funds for that . . . which helped us so much because we each had a wonderful person to help us learn. The nephew of the pastor, Thay (teacher) Quang, had elegant Vietnamese and helped Woody prepare messages and improve on his pronunciation and delivery. Woody became an excellent Vietnamese speaker in his reading and prepared remarks—far better than I was. I spoke more colloquial (country) Vietnamese but could hear and understand more quickly and be understood on a daily level.

A wonderful girl named Co Tuyet lived across the street from us; her father was Chinese and her mother, Vietnamese. They had a big family in a very nice house; when the Americans came they rented it out to a military attaché group, while they themselves lived in lodgings at the back of the house. Tuyet was beautiful, a young and eager Christian believer, with excellent English. She was already a sought-after translator for province visitors when she began to help me in my preparation of materials and messages.

When the Canadian attaché in Hanoi came to Quang Ngai, Tuyet translated for him and he fell in love with her. After a more typical oriental rather than western courtship and engagement, Tuyet and Martin were married in Saigon at the International Church where Pastor Jim Livingston, who had once lived in Quang Ngai, performed the meaningful Christian ceremony. I was so privileged to attend and see her in her lovely western wedding gown.

The reception, in the Chinese section of Saigon, was steeped in Vietnamese culture. She then wore the traditional Vietnamese red dress, and they served a multi-course banquet to the many guests. Tuyet and Martin made a beautiful couple. Later she followed him in his role as a Canadian Foreign Service officer to many countries where he successfully pursued his career and she has been a wonderful diplomat's wife. Today they are retired in Vancouver; their two sons are grown, and they are very devoted to God, faithful in personal spiritual devotion and active in their church life. Tuyet is also very involved and supportive of the Vietnamese Church in Canada. When you see Tuyet and me together, you would never guess our common bond—the wild and wonderful little province of Quang Ngai which formed and influenced us both so deeply and gave me another lifelong friendship.

During one of our Sunday night Bible studies with other expatriates, I got a sudden sharp pain in my mid-section. I screamed and immediately felt a hot enervating sensation that caused me to weaken and slip from my chair to the tile floor, all in one slow-motion minute. The Bible study came to a halt. I could barely respond and no one knew what had happened. Woody ran across the street to call a Spanish doctor who was working for a U.S. civilian agency. Randy, my army nurse girlfriend, ran for her stethoscope and blood pressure cuff and came back. Since I was too weak to even get on the bed, and the cool tiles felt so good, I stayed on the floor. The doctor tried to get down on the floor to get my blood pressure. He was mad. He threw the cuff across the room swearing that it was broken and that he had worked in the worst slums in the world and never had to get down on the floor. I had heightened awareness of everything happening around me but not enough energy to respond.

Woody made the diagnosis; "a ruptured tubal pregnancy," he said. We had experienced one of those before when he was in seminary; he came home to find me unconscious in the bathroom of our little apartment. By now they realized the equipment was not faulty; I had no pulse or blood pressure distinctive enough to register. Knowing there was no blood in the hospital next door, someone in the room made the decision to take me to Chu Lai or Danang. They called the base ambulance, bundled me into it on the stretcher, took me to the helicopter pad, and lifted me on. Meanwhile, Woody had asked a soldier from Chu Lai, who was taking his R&R for a few days at our house, to watch baby Stewart who was just over 7 months old, with the help of the Vietnamese girl currently helping us. Woody walked out on our guests and made it on to the ambulance and helicopter with me; I was only vaguely aware of his presence.

Because of the haste and the noise, the chopper crew had no idea what was wrong with me. They assumed I was pregnant as by now my abdomen was greatly distended and taut. They kept telling me to breathe deep and hold the baby and feeling for contractions; I could only scream as they touched me. After we lifted off, one corpsman turned on a light to start an IV, but the chopper immediately took gunfire so he had to turn off the light. Trying to stop at Chu Lai base, the medivac helicopter was turned away when the base radioed that they had no way to help females. After about 30 minutes in the air, during which time I was in and out of consciousness, we arrived at the Navy Hospital in Danang on China Beach.

Everybody went into action, I was rushed into the triage section where shifts were changing and all the men wanted to see their first female patient. Some started an IV, some took my pressure, and one yelled, "She's gone. She's gone.

No vitals." I could hear and smell it all but I could not even move my tongue a twitch or blink my eyes to let them know I was still inside. They plunged a needle in my hugely distended abdomen and pulled out blood, concluding that Woody's diagnosis was correct.

I heard Woody give them my blood type as they opened my jugular vein and actually pumped the cold blood into me trying to revive me; it worked. I began shivering uncontrollably and within a few minutes could nod my head. I heard Woody give permission to operate as they informed him that this would likely mean no more children. The next thing I knew I heard my name called and male nurses telling me to wake up; my surgery was over. I was in a hospital bed in a small room with tubes coming out of me at many junctures, but I could see and hear and taste and smell and feel, and that felt good. Soon the doctor came in to tell me the good news. I could still have more children. It didn't sound like such good news at the moment.

I remember my recovery as a great time. As soon as I was awake and alert, Woody went back to Quang Ngai, rescued Stewart and brought him to Danang to stay with our colleagues, the Josephsens, who came daily to see me. The hospital beds, all in wards, had no place for women at that time, so they cleaned out a storeroom for me. They had a sign on the door which read, "No swearing, woman patient." I heard many guys go by and swear about whose idea the sign was, push open the door, and then gasp when they saw me. Every day the doctor said I had to take a long walk on the beach so all the corpsmen volunteered to be my caregiver for the day.

My doctors were true professionals; one, a Harvard-trained obstetrician, wondered what he was doing in Vietnam. He wrote up my strange case for medical journals, in fact. It seemed that during my first ectopic pregnancy the affected tube was removed and it left a little dog-eared flap in my uterus. This pregnancy took root in that flap and as it grew, it actually ruptured through the uterine wall which explains why I bled so profusely and quickly. An easy condition to fix, my doctor declared, but only if I got to a surgeon in time. My other doctor had just been featured on the cover of *Life* magazine for removing a live mortar round from the chest of a Vietnamese soldier. The operating room had been completely sandbagged; the doctor and a bomb-squad person were the only ones inside to open the chest, remove and disable the mortar, and thus become heroes. He showed me the amazing x-ray. I was a "piece of cake" after that.

The USO sent several celebrities that stopped by the wards while I recuperated. Whenever one arrived, the guys would wheel me out of my room to sit in a chair of honor. I remember Raymond Burr and Johnny Weismuller, for some reason, probably because Johnny taught us all to do the Tarzan yell. My Doctor released me in time to go to Josephsen's for Thanksgiving dinner; I don't know when I have ever had more reason to celebrate with thanks. More than a year later I found out that a woman in Pennsylvania had been moved to pray for me one day. When comparing dates and hours it was just when I was hovering between life and death in that helicopter, and too weak to cry out for myself, that she interceded for me. Yes, we were uncommonly thankful that year.

CHAPTER ELEVEN

Chaplains donate motorbikes to Pastors

The PALERMO BROS.

Martin & Tuyết

June 66

MRS. AM

HOLIDAYS

Holidays in Vietnam fell into three categories; the ones we shared with both cultures such as Christmas and Easter; the ones that we celebrated only as Americans such as Thanksgiving and January First; and the strictly Vietnamese ones such as Tet, or Lunar New Year. And I love celebrating, so we entered into them all!

During the first year in Danang for language study, we became very homesick. It did not seem at all like Christmas since the Vietnamese in general did not celebrate the occasion. No city lights or decorations brightened the neighborhood; no time off work; no carols in the air; no frenzy of buying and wrapping gifts and no decorated trees. The exception to the rule was the Christian churches, The church's celebrations centered entirely around the birth of Jesus. All throughout the country the Tin Lanh churches had the same theme. It changed each year but always included a Bible text and a suggested mural. They prepared a huge program in every church including a message, choirs from all age groups, and colored lights in the front. As years passed they began decorating trees as well. Very often the program included a pageant depicting the Christmas story. They used

Christmas as a great opportunity to invite friends and neighbors to hear the Good News.

The main church in Danang held their program on Christmas Eve, and, since everyone wanted to visit all the programs, the other ten churches had to have theirs on another afternoon or evening. In addition each church had its worship service on Christmas morning. You could go to programs daily for days before Christmas and sometimes one or two days after, depending on the number of churches in your area. We always had our own "family" Christmas on the first "program-free" day after December twenty-six.

Though we had only been in language study for about two months when we celebrated our first Christmas, Woody was invited to sing a duet for the main program with his co-worker Orrel. They sang, *O Little Town of Bethlehem* in Vietnamese and, since the tune was the same and the words phonetic, it actually worked. I can remember them practicing and me writing home to an incredulous family that it really happened.

That first year a new church across the river in *An Hai*, a Danang "suburb" on China Beach, also invited Woody to give the Christmas morning message through an interpreter. We rode our bicycles through a normal bustling workday crowd on a hot 80 degree morning down to the "people ferry" docked on our side of the Bach Dang River. We jumped on to this big, broad-bottomed skiff clutching our bikes and hanging on to each other while we were rowed across the wide river in about ten minutes Then we jumped off with our bikes ... a feat everyone else seemed to consider normal. We pedaled down dusty roads through a lightly inhabited area to the lovely new church all by itself on a sandy stretch of land near China Beach.

To our surprise the church was full of people and they organized a wonderful full-scale program complete with choirs, lights, a pageant, and a great Christmas message (at least the English side I could understand). We had dinner with the pastor and his family, and the interpreter and then repeated our bikes-across-the-river adventure to get back home. I can still feel the joy of that very different holiday for us, and the warmth of sharing the wonderful story of Christmas across cultures.

After we moved to Quang Ngai, holidays were much the same and we loved going from church to church for the programs. But during Christmas 1967, a very different event took place. A young Korean soldier came to our home one day in early December and introduced himself as David Choo, the soldier-in-charge of a strategic hamlet in the mountains of Quang Ngai province known as Tra Bong. Because of the heavy fighting in the remote areas of the province, the Vietnamese government had brought about 7000 ethnic Vietnamese together into this area where they lived in simple refugee style housing in an area enclosed with bamboo fencing. A small squad of 12 Korean soldiers guarded the perimeter.

The roads to this distant area had become impassable and unsafe so all transport was done by helicopter when supplies or medical help were needed. We were astonished to learn of David's love for these people and his high feeling of responsibility for them. He had already organized schools and a local sort of Council of Elders. He represented far more than the military presence of the Blue Dragon Brigade. David was a believer in Jesus and he could not find anyone in his beloved "hermit kingdom," as he called it, who recognized that name.

So David knocked on our door, totally unknown to us, but aware that we were the "local missionaries," and he presented us with a full-blown plan. First, he shared his disappointment that he never heard singing or music in his village. He wanted to buy a small pump-organ, then have us find someone to go live there and teach the children to play it. Then he wanted someone to organize a singing group and teach the people folk songs and Christmas music. Finally, he would plan a big Christmas program and invite the church young people to come with their choir ending with Woody giving the Christmas story and inviting these people who had never heard of Jesus to follow Him. He told us he would take us in and out via helicopters and we should bring twenty to thirty people. We had never seen such zeal.

Over the next few weeks the plan unfolded; David got the organ but no one volunteered to go live in remote and dangerous Tra Bong. So he decided to make the Christmas program a time to present, demonstrate, and dedicate the organ to the village, and then the village would choose two young people to come down and live in our "white house" student hostel and study organ in Quang Ngai. The date was set and about fifteen young people prepared choir music. One soloist was chosen. The church organist would go and play for the occasion and then teach the selected students back in town. The pastor would go, but Woody would give the message. We all prayed and got very excited.

On the appointed day, we went to the landing pad out near the brigade headquarters, and to our shock, a big crowd was waiting for us. Down came two Chinook helicopters; the transport type of chopper with double rotors and seating for about forty passengers each. Our group took up most of one: Korean military brass and reporters filled the other. We flew about thirty minutes into the mountains and then we landed on top of a cleared area with a spectacular, panoramic view of a range of forested mountains. And then the welcoming committee came. There were dozens of children singing and dancing and placing leis around our necks—not a Vietnamese custom that I had ever seen. They had no more idea of what to expect than we did, but they were very well prepared.

They led us to a flattened and swept area where about forty folding chairs had been placed for the officers and for our visiting group; we were the dignitaries. The seven thousand Vietnamese sat politely on the ground waiting for us. I could not help but think of the feeding of the five thousand as the Bible describes it. Unbelievably, the children sang wonderful songs in the Korean language; they danced and twirled banners and enthralled all those present. Then the time came for David to present the organ. Very few, if any there, had seen one before. The young woman organist obligingly played several numbers on it. The village elders introduced the two young boys who were chosen to come home with us and study organ.

David, through an interpreter, told the people a bit about Christmas and how it was the most important story they would ever hear. The choir sang several carols explained by the pastor. Then a dramatic thing happened. As Miss Na began to sing the beautiful carol "*O Holy Night*," accompanied by the organ, bombers flew across the sky and began to bomb the valley just below us. As we watched the ordnance fall and heard the huge explosions echoing in the valley below, we also heard the beautiful news of the Prince of Peace, the thrill of hope, and the weary world rejoicing because of that newborn babe. The stage was set for Woody to simply tell the Biblical account of the humble birth of the King of Kings. There was absolute silence as he recounted the Christmas story, so familiar to us, but a first hearing for them. No church or cathedral could have been as sacred as that village scene. Then David stood and asked the Council of Elders to join him and Woody, and instructed the others to return to their homes.

I later learned that when they entered their headquarters meeting hall, David told them they needed to believe and asked Woody if they understood. What they told Woody was profound; in essence they said, "We are a traditional people.

We have never heard this message. If this is true, we need to find out and spread the word. But, if this is true, why have we never heard this before? We cannot change on just hearing a message like this once. We need a teacher." Eagerly, David agreed that if we found a pastor to come and live there, he would bring him in and out on the helicopter regularly. This happened.

Meanwhile, as the youth were kicking soccer and takraw balls in the air and showing off the organ, I wanted to go visit with the women. I learned that many of the people had never seen a western woman, and I inspired their curiosity. When I began to speak Vietnamese I got mobbed. They literally pushed-pulled me to their makeshift lean-to homes along the edge of the hill. As I went from house to house, I sat on the bed, which was the only furniture piece they owned. The women gathered around me and listened while I explained why I came to Vietnam. In each of eight to ten one-room dwellings I entered, within a minute someone would appear with a glass full of tea and set it beside me on the bed. They would invite me to drink and I would invite them in return (even though they had none). I would nod, take a drink and set the glass down on the bed. Within a minute it would disappear, only to reappear in the next house upon my arrival there. I realized that the only unstained, uncracked drinking vessel had been given to me and I was humbled beyond measure. We laughed and talked and shared the love and joy of Jesus in Tra Bong. The helicopters came all too soon and took us back to our world, but I will never forget theirs.

The two boys chosen to learn the organ moved into our hostel, ate with the students there, went to school and took organ lessons. They loved being city boys. A few months later they went home for a few weeks for Tet. A pastor had moved up to Tra Bong and was sharing his faith with the eager learners there. He came back to Quang Ngai for Tet. The Viet Cong overran Tra Bong at Tet 68, burned the village to the ground, and no one there escaped. We have no idea what happened to David and his squad, the organ students, or anyone else caught at that fateful time. But we know they heard Good News at least once in their lives, thanks to the irrepressible David Choo.

The church also celebrated Easter. On one memorable Easter Sunday morning in Quang Ngai the young people got us up before dawn and we went in a procession of mopeds, bicycles, Lambros and our van way down the highway into the countryside. We climbed a low hill covered with lots of big rocks, and as dawn broke, we saw Scripture verses painted on all the rocks. "He is not here, He is risen," "Why seek ye the living among the dead?" "Because He lives, we too shall live" and many more. As we stood there with those wonderful affirmations of faith on stone and in hearts, we felt like we were in heaven. Realistically, we stood deep in Viet Cong territory, but, on that day, that hill belonged to God.

We always loved it when our mission chairman came to visit, and I was especially delighted when he brought his wife. On another Easter we were honored to have Grady and Evelyn Mangham visit us in Quang Ngai so we planned a full program. The first event was a Good Friday meeting out in the country at Nghia Hung Church where I spoke. My topic was "Who crucified Jesus?" and I worked so hard to get my point across. Although the Manghams were very gracious about my language ability, I don't think the brevity or the clarity of my lesson impressed the audience. The pastor and wife were honored to have us there and the people of the church hosted a delicious meal.

Saturday evening we had a celebration service at our Quang Ngai Church with lots of music. Grady and Evelyn, who are very musical, insisted we do a quartet together. Woody sings well, but I absolutely do not. I don't know how many in the audience realized only three of the four actually sang; the other one was only lip syncing. Grady preached on Easter Sunday morning to a packed audience commemorating the risen Christ. After a dinner with the pastor and governing board, we prepared for our final weekend plan.

Pastor Chau in Binh Son had told us of a large group of new believers in a fishing village on the coast near the mouth of the Quang Ngai River. He had promised the group that we would try to come on Easter Sunday. A military chaplain procured a helicopter ride for Grady and Woody and they flew there in the mid-afternoon. The chopper pilot put them down and said he would return in two hours. As Grady and Woody left the landing pad, a few believers ran up to them and said, "You have to leave right now. There has just been a big battle and the VC have killed a lot of Americans right here on the beach. We cannot have our service." Well, the helicopter was gone, so Grady and Woody gathered some Christians and had a time of sharing and prayer. The whir of the returning helicopter was sweet music and they returned to Quang Ngai safely with their unbelievable story.

It seems that whenever things were tense, God would bring laughter into our lives in an unusual way. That weekend was no exception due to the cyclo ride Evelyn and I took down to the church—Woody and Grady had gone earlier in the van. We could only find one driver to hail when it was time to go, but he insisted he could get us both in one vehicle. Then he got on back with his small, scrawny body and muscular legs and proceeded to pedal us down the road calling out loudly, "Look here. You will see the strongest man in the world. Look at these two big American women. I am pushing them with no trouble at all. I am the strongest man in the world." These loud declarations were briefly punctuated with drinks from a bottle in his pocket. This continued the entire mile to the church. We laughed so hard at the sideshow we were creating that we could barely talk. Whenever Evelyn and I met each other after that we would say, "Remember when we met the strongest man in the world?"—and follow this with gales of laughter.

When it came to our birthdays and anniversaries, we made a big deal of them with cakes and some special gift from the local shops. Woody began to collect the *"Long Life"* or health figurine, so we always knew what to get him. It was the only one sold alone of the *"Phuoc, Loc, Tho"* trio. These health, wealth, and happiness sets came in all mediums; marble, jade, wood, glass, pewter, and ceramics, and could be purchased all over Asia. These are not religious figures, but carry cultural significance. No matter what size, material, or level of intricacy they are, *Long Life* will always have a bulging bald brow, a cane in one hand, and a pomegranate in the other. One Christmas the Danang Church gave him a beautiful pink marble *"Ong Tho"* from the famed Marble Mountain in Danang.

We tried to serve pork roast at New Year's, give valentines on the proper day, honor our mothers on Mother's Day and keep in mind the American holidays as we could, but often they slipped by unnoticed. However, no matter what holidays we may have forgotten, there would come one hot fall day every year when Woody would announce, "Today is opening day for hunting season in PA." This mark of the seasons was impossible to duplicate unless you considered the gunshot sounds which constantly accompanied our lives in Quang Ngai.

CHAPTER TWELVE

Off to Church

hand-embroidered
gift to Char
from prison women

1967 precious tree

Orrel &
Woody
sing a
duet

Giáo sĩ Stemple

David Choo and the
two organ students

American Holiday

TET '68

*T*et is the Vietnamese word for the vibrant and festive Lunar New Year. In 1968 it happened to be *Tet Mau Than*, or beginning of the year of the Monkey—one of the animals in the twelve-year zodiac cycle. The date of Tet fluctuates every year according to the Lunar calendar. It is like every American holiday rolled into one. It combines the gift giving of Christmas, the fireworks of July 4, the big family meal of Thanksgiving, the return of spirits of Halloween, the new beginnings of Easter, and the flowers of springtime. It is also everyone's birthday.

Traditionally, Vietnamese figure age differently from the western way. At birth, the Vietnamese child is one; at the next Tet the child turns two; and then every New Year thereafter he adds a year like everyone else. So, it is theoretically possible for a Vietnamese child to be "two" when he was only a month old if he were born near Tet. At the very least he would always be counted one year older than the western child born on the same day. Originally Tet was celebrated for as many as ten days, but in "our time" it lasted three long, fun-filled celebratory days.

Actually, the entire month before Tet involved everyone in feverish activity. All houses and properties had to be cleaned and swept inside and out; this almost always included a fresh coat of light tan or pastel "whitewash" swept on houses, fences, gates, stores, schools, and hospitals. Everybody got a new set of clothing; all debts were paid, and food was prepared for the entire holiday. Ironically, crimes like theft escalated that month as people looked for ways to pay their obligations. All households bought a real or artificial plant or branch of an apricot or peach tree with yellow blossoms and put it in a pot or vase in the house. It looked a lot like forsythia: this indicated the early spring flowers. If real, it needed to blossom by Tet and the more the buds, the better the "luck." Often Tet greeting cards would be hung on the tree and also passed on as greetings to officials and friends.

Some of the old customs rooted in Confucian teachings and ancestor veneration may not have been believed, but the Vietnamese continued to observe them as tradition dictated. These customs included scaring the evil spirits away with fireworks at midnight on Tet "eve," not scolding children for three days as it would predict how your year would go, being horrified if a dish or glass broke since this also meant bad luck for the year, doing no work during the holiday, and generally avoiding any negative things so that you would have a positive year.

Everybody returned to their family home for the three days. Transportation was nearly unobtainable the week before Tet, as people scrambled to arrive home for the big meal New Year's Eve. Decorated shops continued to sell gifts, candy and special foods even during the war years. Each year during the war, both sides declared a one week truce so that the military could get home for a few days and shoot off a little ammunition at midnight, even though it was forbidden. Markets would be closed for three days, so everything had to be prepared ahead of time.

Visiting during Tet is *the* big deal. The first visitor to cross your threshold New Year's Day became the predictor for the year, so we were told never to visit until the afternoon of Day One. In Quang Ngai we always went with Pastor and Mrs Chau and the elders of the church to call on church members beginning at noon, and we visited non-stop the next two days. People in the church would give us the traditional *banh tat* which the women had spent the previous weeks making. These sticky rice rolls were about a foot long and three inches in diameter with beans or sausage in the center wrapped in banana leaves and steamed for hours. They were unwrapped and sliced to serve with a sort of pickled vegetable mixture. We never told our Vietnamese friends that we liked them best fried with my home-made maple syrup on them.

Best of all, children received bright red little envelopes with new paper money in them if they bowed politely and greeted the adults in the home. Stewart loved doing this, and we garnered more envelopes than we gave out once he came along with us!

Tet Mau Than (the Year of the Monkey) started the usual way. We had been given about twenty rolls of *Banh Tat* and lots of candied fruit. We readied our new money and envelopes to give out, and had small gifts of candy for the households we would visit. Our house helper had gone home to the countryside and the students in our backyard hostel had taken off for their homes. New Year's Eve was very quiet until midnight when lots of "illegal" fireworks and shooting broke the silence for a brief celebration. The Tet truce was in place so the military were almost non-existent at the base across the street and the customary helicopter landings next to us had come to a stop, if only temporarily.

When morning came, we went to meet the pastor and wife and paid our obligatory calls on the province chief and district officials. About noon we gathered with the elders and church officers to visit homes of church families. At every spot there was something special to eat, but always the bright red watermelon seeds and dried candied fruit, called *muc*, of which the pink, green and white coconut strips were my favorite. Late in the afternoon we went back to the church. Pastor Chau and the elders quite solemnly told us that they felt things were too quiet, and they suspected trouble. They told us to go home and bar our windows and doors and not come out to visit any more that evening or even the next day. This surprised and shocked us.

As we drove our van home we noticed the eerie afternoon quiet; no vehicles, no walking together as families, no happy visiting, not even any local radio service. When we got home we pulled the wooden shutters closed over our windows and secured the wooden bars on our doors. Quang Ngai waited, but not for long. About midnight a huge bombardment began and we could hear shouting and lots of small arms fire in the street, as well as commotion and activity in the hospital next door. We got Stewart and sat in our bunker, later returning to our bed.

At daybreak we cautiously opened our shutters but could see nothing happening; Woody went next door to the hospital to see if he could help with the wounded, but they quickly sent him home whispering that the Viet Cong had taken over the hospital as well as the radio station and province center. Quang Ngai was under Viet Cong control.

Then the unthinkable; we finally got the news broadcasting from FEBC in Manila and heard that five of our missionary colleagues had been killed in the mountain town of Banmethuot. We held each other and wept. Why were our lives spared and our precious friends taken? What we thought was a local skirmish was a well planned and coordinated truce-breaking attack on every province center in the south, including the bold attack on the American embassy in Saigon. We were small fish, totally out of contact and unsure what to do. Even our pastor could not get down the road to us, we later learned. Further news from Banmethuot told of Marie Ziemer's rescue and the capture of my dear friend Betty Olsen and two others. We stayed glued to the radio.

In the late morning, heavy fighting broke out again and Huey gunships were flying overhead strafing in our neighborhood. The empty shell casings fell like rain on our roof. Neighbors who lived in the sugar cane fields behind us came running to get into our house which was more substantial. About thirty of us huddled in the living room and each time the planes made a pass we fell to the floor and covered our heads. Stewart followed along, happily singing, "Ashes, ashes, all fall down." Woody, meanwhile, climbed the ladder to our water tower trying to see the location of the battle.

A few hours later, during a lull in the fighting, the neighbors went home and the loud-speaker Lambro trucks rattled down the street with their familiar "Chu Y, Chu Y" (Pay attention) announcements which were usually advertising movies or local news. This time they asked for food for the government soldiers since all markets were closed and they had no way to prepare food for the hastily-called fighting men. I ran out with my twenty rolls of *banh tat* to donate to the cause of the men of the Vietnamese Second Division, who did eventually retake our town and restore order.

Meanwhile, Woody walked down to see what was happening at the next-door hospital and neighboring prison which was about 200 yards from our house. A huge battle had taken place at the prison as the Viet Cong broke in and tried to "liberate" the prisoners to follow them. More than half of the prisoners had been given home leave for Tet, and of those that remained few wanted to follow these men, who were now "holed up" in the prison. That is why the American air strikes had been called in to shell the prison.

Woody found many dead, black-pajama clad Viet Cong there. They had grenade belts which held grenades made of American discarded soda cans with homemade detonators. They also had hollow bamboo "lunch buckets" stuffed with cooked sticky rice and beans strung around their necks. Woody got photographs of this gruesome scene but we never felt comfortable showing them in public. The prison now was blown wide open, and some of the prisoners, who had followed Jesus the forgiver during our teaching times, came to our house rather than take the opportunity to escape. They stayed in our "white house" hostel by night and went down to the prison to get their meals at mealtime until the prison could be repaired and they would return to finish their sentence.

The day's news had been focused on the breaching and retaking of the U.S. embassy in Saigon with little being reported about outlying towns. That evening FEBC reported that all other C&MA missionaries had been located and were safe. How did they know about us? The end of this second day of Tet found us tense, broken-hearted, and perplexed about what to do in our volatile town, but very thankful we had survived that day's events. If ever we thought about God's calling, it was that day, and we remained sure He was in control.

The next morning, Day Three of Tet, the pastor and church friends came to see us. They rejoiced in our safety but told us the other American aid workers would be leaving town that morning. We felt the worst was over, so we remained cautiously optimistic. About noon a jeep pulled into our driveway and an American soldier came to tell us that our mission had given an order that all women and children had to leave the country for one month; the men could choose to go or stay. Then he said that the only plane in or out of Quang Ngai would be leaving for Danang in thirty minutes and I had to be on it with Stewart. No choice to make; no time to think.

We quickly pulled the cloth diapers off the line and grabbed our small emergency suitcase containing papers, some money, boiled water, some food for Stewart and a change of clothing for us each. We got to the airport just as the plane was ready to take off. I kissed Woody goodbye and he watched me climb the metal stairs with Stewart in one arm and the suitcase in the other. The most important thing I had was his pacifier. It turned out he slept everywhere we went as long as he could locate that pacifier. I wish it were to be as easy for me. I had no idea if I would ever see my beloved husband again, let alone our Quang Ngai home, church family, friends and neighbors.

We got off the plane out onto the Danang tarmac, and I headed toward the terminal, where I hoped to call our colleagues, the Josephsens. But suddenly I heard someone calling my name—there was Nancy Josephsen, hanging out of a C-123 plane door trying to get my attention. They and several other families were being evacuated from Danang to the coastal town of Nhatrang, so we got on that plane to go with them. We sat there over an hour: apparently Vietnamese President Thieu was visiting Nhatrang so nothing was allowed in Nhatrang airspace. It was getting late in the afternoon when the powers-that-be (I never knew who because no one knew what to do with this planeload of civilians) decided to let us go back to town, eat supper, and then gather again at a certain spot in downtown Danang where we would spend the night. So Stewart and I went into town with the Josephsens and we had a quick meal.

I called Woody on our erratic Vietnamese phone system and managed to get a message to him that I had only gotten as far as Danang and if he could, he should hitch a ride to be with us. Miraculously, he was able to catch a helicopter ride and showed up just as we were joining all the other civilians at a hotel which was slated to be a barracks, but was still under construction. We were all assigned rooms and given instructions. We were to keep all children totally under control since the guards were stringing bombs all around the building and anyone would trip the wires if they tried to go in or out. Also, each floor was to have a watchman who would be given a gun to stand watch. Because we got assigned to the floor with all the people doing alternate service, we got the guns in our room—but we did not stay awake. We tucked Stewart into a big dresser drawer on the floor, gave him his pacifier and he slept all night. We held each other and prayed and fell asleep exhausted, but at least together.

The next day Woody went back to Quang Ngai and Stewart and I did fly to Saigon, where we joined the Alliance missionaries from all over Vietnam; we maxed out the guest house. Our American leadership was there and in close contact with the embassy personnel who had said we needed to leave the country for one month, with further evaluation to follow. All non-critical U.S. personnel were to leave, but our missionary men could stay or leave as they wished. Woody wished to stay, and I concurred. When we arrived in Bangkok as front page news – the U.S. war refugees had come. We crammed into our Alliance guest house and other expatriates from all over Bangkok brought clothes, shoes and emergency things. Everyone had his own war story and some families went on home to North America.

Due to the overcrowding, the guest house host asked me to go stay with our Alliance missionaries in Korat, the location of our mission headquarters in central-northeast Thailand. They tempted me by telling me there was a big American base there where I could probably call my husband on the military line. Bill Carlson drove me and Stewart with suitcase and pacifier in tow the six hours to Korat and deposited us on the doorstep of colleagues there.

Much to my great surprise, a missionary family living in Korat had a son working as a military radio operator in Quang Ngai Vietnam. Talk about a small world! He alerted Woody as to when I would call and Woody waited at the base radio room for me to call at the appointed hour. When I talked with him from the Korat base it sounded like he was in the next room. We did this two Monday evenings as I recall and I learned that the situation remained very tense in our town, but Woody was not feeling pressure. During the day Stewart and I read, walked and shopped. The mission gave us funds to buy clothes as most of us left with just one outfit, so I had a stylish Thai silk four- piece outfit made that I wore for years afterward. I had heard about a lovely, inexpensive Christian retreat center on the beach in south Thailand, and inquired about it. I decided to take Stewart there by train.

On the way we stopped in Bangkok for a day. We happened to be arriving in the afternoon just at the time Bonnie Carlson was hosting a tea for the American women's club who had donated so many things to us "refugees." She asked me in advance to speak at the tea, which was to become a big social event. I wore my Thai silk, gave a fun talk of appreciation, and was quoted word-for-word in the next day's *Bangkok Post*. To everyone's surprise, in the middle of my talk a jeep pulled into the yard, two soldiers in fatigues jumped out and came up to interrupt me. They were friends from Quang Ngai on an R&R break to Bangkok. Woody had asked them to look me up and reassure me he was okay as there had been a big battle the night before and a mutual friend of ours, the captain of a helicopter, had been killed. This was an impressive illustration to my talk, and I introduced the guys to everyone there.

Stewart and I spent about ten more days on beautiful Hua Hin beach with miles of fine sand where we sat, walked, played, shelled and fended off wild dogs. I sat and meditated for hours on God's Word, the events of the past weeks, and what God might have for our future. This peaceful seaside retreat was very healing for me, and the boarding-house style homemade meals were a wonderful bonus. At the end of the month Woody met us in Saigon for a *very* happy reunion.

The next day the embassy personnel met with our leaders to talk about our people going back to their stations. That evening we gathered for mission prayers and discussion. In public, the Alliance Vice President for Overseas Ministries said, "The embassy has said that everyone can go back to their stations except for those in Quang Ngai." He did not look at us as he spoke. We were stunned.

We begged and pleaded to our field director to let us go back for the few more months we had before our home assignment. We promised him that if we landed on our little airstrip and one single person who knew us and our ministry, whether American military or Vietnamese, told us it was not safe, we would get back on the plane. He reluctantly agreed. We spent four more wonderful productive months in Quang Ngai.

CHAPTER THIRTEEN

The village to the rear of the prison – hit by V.C.
mortars first, then burned by the V.C. when leaving.
ARVN families lived here. Many were killed.
Tet Quang Ngai 2/68

The village to the rear of the prison
mortared and burned by the V.C. because
they were families of ARVN soldiers.
Many innocent people wounded + killed
Tet 2/68 Quang Ngai

The old prison office where we always drank tea before our services.
Tet '68
Quảng Ngãi

This young boy, maybe 14 or 15 had a satchel charge, but never got to use it. The building behind is the local weather station right outside the prison. Woody always parked right here for prison ministry Tet '68

CHAPTER FOURTEEN

ONE AMAZING TERM

We knew our days in Quang Ngai were numbered. We had tickets to go home in mid-August with plans to travel through Europe for about two weeks to decompress. We would visit five cities for two-and-a-half days each, faithfully following our travel guide, *Europe on five dollars a day*. Meanwhile, we had a lot of work to do.

We had been feverishly working toward the building of a church in a country area called Xuan Quang. One day when Woody visited Chu Lai base he noticed they were extending the runway. To do this, they made test blocks from each batch of cement and used a huge weight to put pressure on them until they cracked; this resulted in big broken half-blocks of heavy duty cement on a discard pile. When Woody inquired and found that they did not have a purpose for those blocks, he requested to use them to build a church.

The construction crew was more than happy to oblige and a Special Forces captain offered a deuce-and-a-half truck to transport them to the site. We had a huge dedication ceremony which was the culmination of much of our ministry in the province, and the main reason we had begged to return. Many of these people were believers because of the original "disastrous" tent meeting we had held when we first came to Quang Ngai. That church building was like a fortress and still stands strong today, as do the believers in that area, who are the "real" church. It was a release for us to see that project completed for God's glory. On the day of the church dedication we had awakened to see eight civilian bodies lying dead in front of our house. The Viet Cong took over the radio station for a few days, but strangely enough, life seemed to continue on. It was bizarre.

Besides the "real" war which continued to rage, a conflict between the Buddhists and the government broke out, mostly over the level of where the Buddhist flag could fly. All over the country there were cases of self-immolation by monks to further Buddhist ideals, and the unrest proliferated in our province. A local monk set fire to himself in downtown Quang Ngai and hundreds turned out for the big funeral with procession up to Buddha Mountain for the burial.

Other civilians returned back to the province after a month post-Tet hiatus. We celebrated the wedding of Earl and Pat who worked effectively with the refugee community. Their ceremony beautifully blended the Vietnamese and American cultures. Pastor Chau donned his traditional formal robe, the *ao dai*, to perform the ceremony; I stood in as "mother" for Pat whose bridesmaids were Vietnamese friends, and Woody did the music (as in, ran the tape recorder).

During the time I was away after Tet, what came to be known as the "My Lai massacre" occurred in our province, just north of Quang Ngai town. My Lai was a heavily controlled Viet Cong area which we had never been able to visit. We did not know the details of the massacre until we read about it in the press. Several years later we actually were questioned by the American military panel investigating the incident to see if we had been aware of it but we did not have any information. We grieved for the loss of life and realized the divided loyalties and feelings represented the typical sentiments of our province villages which took the brunt of the fighting.

One night during heavy fighting, Woody woke up and said, "We need to go across the street." Across the street was a large house which had been rented to U.S. military and civilian nurses; a few Marines, who guarded the house, lived in back. They had one big, windowless room which had been made into a bunker, and each night they pulled a jeep up against their gate to prevent entry. They had guard towers on each of the four corners of the walls. We had been told to come there anytime we felt we needed the security, but so far we had felt safer in our own house where everyone in town knew who we were. So I was surprised and protested when Woody wanted to go.

Woody pulled on a T-shirt and pants, picked up Stewart and our emergency suitcase, and said "Let's go." I threw on a robe and followed him. A strange eeriness had fallen over the neighborhood. There were no sounds at all and no one in the street. Flares fell from unseen planes illuminating the night as day. I felt like we were combatants in a western like *High Noon*, coming down a street knowing people were watching and waiting for something to happen. As we neared the gate we heard someone backing the jeep away from it, so we knew we had been seen from the guard towers. The gate opened in front of us and we scurried in and rushed to the bunker where the house occupants had already gathered.

Almost immediately a huge battle broke out and we sat waiting. By morning all gunfire stopped, and we cautiously looked out the gate to see that morning traffic had begun to circulate like any normal day. When we went back into our house we saw that a bullet had gone through our living room and lodged in a wall; the only time that the war breached the interior of our house.

One time there had been severe fighting in the town and mortar rounds had landed all around our property. One had hit next door in the hospital and a B-40 rocket had actually gone through the gate across the street, smashing through the vehicle parked there. In the empty field to the other side of us more mortar rounds had hit, and some had even started a fire in the sugar cane fields behind us. Afterwards a chaplain friend of ours brought a helicopter over our property to take pictures of the battle results: they were dramatic. There were obvious craters all around our property, but it was like the angels had spread a tent over our little square bounded by the coconut trees. Our house and our property remained unscathed.

One other time when Stewart and I were away a few days, there was severe fighting and Woody went across the street. The nurses who lived there were so glad to see him as they were very tense and frightened. They told him they saw a Viet Cong trying to get into their upstairs rooms from a balcony. They insisted he go upstairs so they could show him the suspicious window; sure enough, he saw a form outside. The one nurse cocked a pistol and told Woody to throw open the French door. He was so scared of her that he did it. A Viet Cong? Not really; it was a drunken American Marine trying to find the nurses. Woody took him to his superior, thankful neither he nor the Marine got shot.

Also during these final months, more and more U.S. troops became aware of our presence and wanted to help in our ministry. They raised money for a motorbike for each of the five country pastors; they imported little pump organs and simple public address systems for the churches. It was a revelation to them to see all that was going on other than fighting in that war-torn province.

Our annual conference was the highlight of the year for us as we joined together with all our team for a week of relaxation, spiritual and physical renewal, eating good food, and visiting with those we hadn't seen for a year. Counting men, women and preschool children there would be about eighty of us. A special speaker would come from the U.S. or Canada to teach God's Word, and it always seemed to be the right person for the right time.

We had allocations for the next year's assignments, elections of our chairman and committees, reports from every station, proper business, softball games and a "fun night" that was a highlight of the year. I can remember corny jokes, take-offs on one another, and a spoof on "Laugh-In" that will live on in history. But the most precious and poignant memory to me was the singing. We had LOTS of good musicians among our missionaries and they were divided into choirs, solos, duet-trios-quartets, instrumental numbers— and every combination you can imagine. The final event of every conference was a group song led by Grady Mangham. It was called "The Coming of His Feet," and we were a giant choir watching Grady's every move.

The first verse was at regular tempo; *"In the crimson of the morning, In the whiteness of the noon, In the amber glory of the day's retreat; In the midnight robed in darkness, Or the gleaming of the moon—I listen for the coming of His Feet."*

Verses 2, 3, and 4 each had singular direction which we all followed and then came the hushed and slow final verse, filling us with promise; *"He is coming, O my spirit, With His everlasting peace,"* (pause then rising in volume); *"with His blessedness immortal and complete;*

He is coming, "(draw out next three words) *"O—my—spir—it, And His coming brings release—I—listen"* (abrupt stop, pause, then resume in triumph); *"for the coming of His feet."*

None of us who served in Vietnam in those years will forget the tense moments or the camaraderie among workers. Our team and the wonderful Vietnamese pastors and wives we worked with were truly "a band of brothers."

I was pregnant with our second son Sam those last months we were in Quang Ngai, and much more relaxed about this pregnancy. We arrived home to a far different America from the one we had left, but we also found people aware of what we had been doing and full of faith and prayer for the "other news" from Vietnam.

We didn't know it then, but we would not be reassigned to Quang Ngai when we returned to Vietnam because the Vietnamese church requested a different assignment for us. Yes, another amazing four years awaited us in the city of Danang.

CHAPTER FOURTEEN

Annual Conference

Pastor Châu and family say good bye at airport

Church Leaders

Woody preaching

Church Dedication

PART TWO

D A N A N G

Charlotte and Woody Stemple
Sammy and Stewart

CHAPTER 15

RETURN TO DANANG

W e had a wonderful year of furlough living right on Lake Erie in my parents' cottage at a Christian retreat center called Beulah Beach. Being near both sets of families allowed us to enjoy both being in their homes and having them visit us in ours. All of us especially savored the peace and beauty of our setting and the change of the four seasons. We took lots of slide pictures of colored leaves, snow and ice, blossoming fruit trees, and especially sunsets over the lake. Sledding down the hill onto the frozen lake seemed as far as one could be from the hot beaches and rice paddies of Vietnam.

The highlight of our year was the birth of Samuel Cox Stemple on December 18, 1968 by C-section in the Barberton Ohio Hospital. The name Samuel came from the biblical baby who was so greatly desired by his parents which means, "Asked of God." Cox is Woody's mother's family name which we wanted to honor, especially since Grandma Cox was our only living grandparent. Sam and I came home to my mom and dad's house in Akron just in time for Christmas. It was a wonderful celebration with family and friends and all the family customs we had missed for four years. We sent a Western Union telegram to Quang

Ngai to let Pastor and Mrs. Chau know of Sam's birth. They sent one back with their congratulations and asking to name Samuel with a Vietnamese name. Of course we consented, so his Vietnamese name is *Nghia Hung*. *Nghia* represents the old spelling of Quang Ngai province, and *Hung* is part of the word for "revival"as in, *Phuc Hung*. The pastor prayed a blessing over the name; that Sam would bring revival to many people even as the prophet Samuel in the Bible. His telegram made us so homesick for Vietnam.

Woody, as required by our mission, spent two eight-week "tours" visiting assigned churches and giving news of our activity in Vietnam. The fall odyssey took him to Minnesota and the Dakotas; the spring tour was in Ontario, Canada. We actually joined him in a few places there. These tours not only encouraged financial support to our mission, but gave us many new friends and people who began to pray for our ministry. This was invaluable to us. Other than that, our "home" churches in the Erie and Akron areas invited us to speak, and I shared our stories with many women's groups. Vietnam was a popular topic and everyone wanted to hear about our work there including radio stations, service clubs, and families of servicemen. We hauled the boys along and Stewart willingly said a few things in Vietnamese which the people enjoyed hearing. Most people, very conversant with the news reports from Vietnam, expressed their surprise and delight to hear how God was working in the church of Vietnam; a decidedly different approach than the usual nightly news.

Wherever we spoke that included a question-answer session, the number one question was, "What do you think about the war?" That issue polarized our nation and we lived in the midst of it. We tried to stay non-political and focus on our little part of the situation and what we believed God was doing there, because there were no easy answers. One night we consented to be on an all-night live call-in TV show in the Pittsburgh area. Staring into the cameras, we tried to react to all the questions with professional ease, but we will not forget the man who called with a very belligerent question. He yelled into the phone, "What was the reverend doing down on his knees when Americans were dying—get up and fight like a man!" Thankfully, the host stepped in with a comment followed by a commercial ... and we quit the TV business.

The year went by all too quickly and we began to gather our belongings to prepare for our return to Quang Ngai. We packed our things in fifty-gallon steel drums, which were trucked to a port, sent by ship to Saigon and then trans-shipped up to Danang. This time we were more knowledgeable about what we could get and needed in Vietnam, so only packed items that could only be found in the U.S., plus a few sentimental things.

Surviving the packing tested our marriage; Woody told me to put everything in one place that I wanted packed; he loved fitting them in like a jigsaw puzzle and was very creative in getting things into those round containers. He cut the handle off my good broom so it would fit, then devised a sleeve to put it back together when we arrived. We never did put it back together as the Vietnamese use those wonderful, short soft brooms that work so much better. He put all the lamp shades in and packed around them. When he unrolled toilet paper to use as packaging for our glassware, I knew I would be rolling it back up for precious soft use on arrival. I remember what he did to several boxes of table games I chose to take. I was unaware that he would not like the big boxes taking up so much space, so he dumped all the pieces, dice, figures, paper money, and parts of about ten different games into one plastic bag. I had a fit when we got there, but actually, we had as much fun sorting the parts as we did playing the games.

When he began to question the need for things I had chosen, life got interesting. I reminded him my part was to choose; his was to pack. I insisted I did not need to justify every single item; if I wanted it, I wanted it! He seemed to agree, but months later when I couldn't find objects as we unpacked in Vietnam, I realized he had just hidden the things he did not want to pack and left them in the U.S. Welding the drums shut brought an end to the drama. That is, until we got there and realized we had welded shut the tools inside as well and had to find a creative way to get the things back out. Opening the drums made it like Christmas in our new home half a world away.

Our new home—we expected to return to Quang Ngai; Pastor Chau and our friends there were counting the days. Meanwhile, during our annual Field Conference that took place in Dalat, Vietnam, the all-powerful group of co-workers called, "The Allocations Committee," met to decide the ministry place for each missionary unit (couple or single). Their intention was to send us back to our beloved town, but it was discovered that there was no one available to go to the city of Danang that coming year. The Vietnamese church, as well as our mission, could not leave that place unfilled by missionaries.

Danang was the "mother church;" the place where the Gospel first came to Vietnam. The district superintendent lived there and supervised all the churches in the provinces of Qui Nhon, Quang Ngai, Quang Nam, Thua Thien, and Quang Tri. This included the old imperial capital of Hue and north to the border dividing line with North Vietnam. This church regional area was called Central Vietnam and actually approximated the military division called "I Corps," with headquarters in Danang. The mission property included apartments for all the new missionaries as they did their obligatory Vietnamese language study. The large main house also had guest rooms to house mission leaders and friends from cooperating agencies who came there for visits since no suitable hotels were available at the time. There "had to be" a missionary there.

There had "always been" a missionary who lived next to the large Central Danang Tin Lanh church, and the pastor and family were next-door neighbors. The property also housed a large Christian high school which had once been the Bible school until it was relocated outside the coastal city of Nhatrang. In other words, Danang represented the center of all Protestant Gospel (Tin Lanh) activity and needed missionary oversight far more than Quang Ngai town. So, our missionary colleagues at Conference appointed us to Danang and we received a telegram informing us of the fact.

We could have complained or resisted. In fact, I think we did. Our biggest concern was that this move removed us one step from the people we dearly loved. Instead of working directly with the people alongside our Vietnamese pastors, we would be working with the superintendent and pastors; training and resourcing them to be effective. It would be more administrative, and we would be under more scrutiny with more bosses, or so it seemed to us. But we have always believed in "constituted authority," so we prayed about it, agreed to it, and arrived for the second time in the city of Danang—this time as "head of station."

CHAPTER FIFTEEN

Our house (back view)

Josephsens – Huế

Drummonds Quảng Ngãi

Stedmans lang. study

CHAPTER 16

RELATIONSHIPS

The Danang church waited for our arrival and warmly welcomed us. For us, the social network was very different and we had to learn our place all over again. Our "counterpart," to use the current military term, was Pastor Vong, the District Superintendent. He usually dealt with much more experienced missionaries than we were but he gave us his early blessing. He had his offices just around the corner and he took Woody with him to introduce him to the pastors and churches as he visited them. Mr. Vong had a history of standing for his faith in the French-Indochinese conflict and was a bold and courageous believer. We understood that Woody's presence was often "used" as leverage with American Chaplains who wanted to donate to the various churches, and also to drive Pastor Vong to places at certain times, but he also supported us and gave freedom and legitimacy to ministries we initiated on our own.

His family also became friends, especially his daughter and son-in-law who was pastor at a thriving church/school/medical complex just at the end of the busy Danang runway. Many times we sat in that church and counted the bombers as they took off; then counted them as they returned, always happy when we tallied the same number. The take-offs were a distraction to the message, and often the speaker had to stop while we waited for the loud planes to get away, but it soon became just another aspect of life in that crowded noisy port city. One of Mr. Vong's sons had been rebellious in his early teens, and had scrawled "Missionary Go Home" on the wall of the mission house a few years before we had arrived. Now he was older, and was to become totally transformed during a revival at the Bible College; all those early passions now already useful in the church. The youngest son befriended our sons in the children's program. Today, unbelievably, he is the respected pastor of the huge, rebuilt Danang church which has made us all so delighted. This family impacted us immensely in our next four years.

Woody and Pastor Vong disagreed on a few things, but the love of God and of each other kept us from a split in relationship. When we first arrived, he told Woody (with a gleam in his eye and a grin on his face) that all the missionaries who had been former "head of station" had given their tithe to the district. Without missing a beat, Woody responded (with a grin on his face) that when God told him where to give his tithe, he would obey, and that perhaps Pastor Vong would pray it would be the district. Nothing was ever said on that subject again. A few years later Pastor Vong told Woody he would have to choose between the established church and a sort of breakaway group of youth who were very effective with social work. Woody did not respond immediately and God gave him the wisdom to walk with and support both groups without offending either. This also was to lead to remarkable advance of the Gospel through meeting social needs in the coming days, to the glory of God.

One of the highlights of our entire life in Vietnam was the Lunar New Year's Eve when Pastor Vong personally came and invited us to come and share the meal with his family—the most intimate event in family life. As we sat and prayed on the eve of that Tet Holiday, we felt fully accepted in spite of the multitude of language and cultural barriers, and realized anew that "love covers a multitude of sins," as the Bible says.

Another key family in our lives turned out to be the family of the Danang church pastor who lived next door to us. Their parsonage sat at the side of the church, as in most cases in Vietnam. Only a double driveway separated us from them so we got to know who was visiting, what they were doing, and when they were home, and vice versa. Their children played with ours as good friends and we all moved easily between their house, the church, and our house. For a time Woody taught Pastor Minh English and they established a wonderful relationship.

Often when Woody would be with Pastor Minh, either sitting next to him or walking alongside him, Pastor would rub Woody's arm or take his hand in friendship. At first, this was difficult due to our own cultural implications, but later we realized the acceptance and friendship this indicated. It became second nature to walk hand-in-hand, unless of course, an American soldier happened to come by, in which case Woody would subtly withdraw his hand.

We easily moved into the spacious, airy house. We had a large bedroom right off the dining room with the children's smaller bedroom off of ours. The dining room held a table which could serve 20 easily. We ate at one end when it was "just us," but there were usually more. The living room was very large with a fireplace we made good use of during the three "winter months," which were basically chilly and rainy. Its chief advantage was to dry clothing which we rotated on racks in front of it. Of course, the rest of the year clothing dried quickly on outside lines.

The other side of the living room was a mirror image of our bedroom side; one smaller bedroom and one larger one with a complete bathroom at the back. This was Danang's "best hotel." A closed-in front porch ran the length of the front which included my office on one side and Woody's on the other. No one used the front door which technically opened onto the main street. It had a hedge and fence along the front and a squatter's market on the outside of the fence. A closed-in back porch ran the length of the back and included a storage hall and a kitchen which was added some years previously when the cooking facilities were moved from "out in back" to inside the house. Everyone entered through the back door and before long an almost constant stream of people were coming or going through it.

Once again, we discovered that "helpers" came along with this house. *Chi Hoa* (Sister Flower) was the cook and general overseer of the house. She lived in back of the garage with her three children—boys named Tuan and Huan and a little girl orphan she had adopted named *Ti*, or "little bit." These children became the inseparable companions of our boys. Chi Hoa was a marvelous cook and baker and could fix American or Vietnamese meals for any number of people on fast notice. It helped that the market was right on our corner. With the number of guests we would be having, she was invaluable. A second helper named Chi Lien cleaned, did laundry and babysat if we were out about town. Our home functioned as efficiently with or without us which freed us for ministry, meetings, office work, studying, mentoring of the new missionaries, and many other things that would come our way over the next years.

We also had a caretaker/yard worker named *Bac Le* (Uncle "Lay"). He was a gracious, faithful man who kept the yard, bushes, trees, and entire property well kept. He loved to graft new varieties of flowers and present them to us. He tended fruit trees or plants and would always bring us the first bloom of a flower, or fruit off a tree. He would present it to us with two hands, ceremonially, and say, *"Trai dau mua thuoc ve chu mua,"* meaning, "The first fruit of the season belongs to the head of the harvest" … a totally biblical concept. We loved it.

One other thing Bac Le taught me was that whenever he received anything from us—whether the weekly pay (always in an envelope), or a small gift, or something to eat—he would receive it with both hands and say, "*Cam on Chua, Cam on Ong Ba.*" This means, "Thanks to God and thanks to you." No matter what happened, great or small, he thanked God before thanking other people. And he was wonderful with the children; always thinking of ways to please them or help them play. He built an imaginative, fairly large tree house in the starfruit tree outside our back door. It had steps up, a floor, sides, roof, windows and a latticed "porch." It would hold up to six kids sitting cross-legged on the floor. The missionary children in Danang and their Vietnamese friends spent many happy hours there.

At one point, Uncle Le informed us he had worked for the mission on that property for almost fifty years and that the anniversary approached. We asked about his history, and he told us this remarkable story. The French gave the property to the mission when the first missionaries came in 1911. During World War I they had to evacuate and when they returned after the war, Uncle Le was hired. During World War II the missionaries were interned in a prison camp in My Tho, South Vietnam and eventually repatriated to the U.S. on a ship named the *Gripsholm*. (Incidentally, the *Gripsholm* was a Swedish cruise ship that had been chartered by the U.S. State Department from 1942-1946 for the purpose of prisoner exchange and repatriation. It carried Japanese and German nationals to exchange points where American and Canadian citizens were picked up to bring them home. The ship made twelve round trips and repatriated a total of 27,712 North Americans, of which history our Vietnam missionaries were a part).

During this time the Japanese occupied Danang and used the mission house and compound as their headquarters. Uncle Le saw that each evening the officers and men partied, drank a lot, and made a big mess in the house and yard. Each day he would go and clean things up very early in the morning. Neighbors asked him if he was working for the Japanese. "No," he said. "Is the mission getting money in to you?" Again, "No, they are not." "Then why are you working so hard day after day if no one is paying you?" they persisted in asking. Uncle Le answered, "I believe the missionaries will come back one day, and I want things in good order when they come." I was struck by the similarity of Jesus' teaching that when he returns he will say to those who have served Him, "Well done, good and faithful servant."

We celebrated his fifty year employment anniversary with a ceremony and letter from the mission for Uncle Le, as well as a gift of living room furnishings for his home above a store just down the street from us. Eventually, after the Communists took over Vietnam in 1975 and all the westerners had to leave the country, we heard that Uncle Le kept up the mission property every day just like he had done for well over fifty years, until the day he died. He truly worked for God and not for Americans. Well done, faithful servant; your life was a message to us.

CHAPTER SIXTEEN

District Committee

Uncle Lê & wife

Pastor Quy and family

185

CHAPTER 17

FRIEND HIEN

Almost immediately upon arrival we were asked to take part in ministries even though our language was rusty from our year away. When one of the dozen or more churches in Danang invited Woody to preach, he would prepare his message in Vietnamese and then go over it with a student or someone who could check his vocabulary and grammar. We found a wonderful young man named Hien who was active in the youth group and excellent in English, as well as conversant with theological terms and biblical concepts. It was a great match.

As Woody worked with Hien, we became very close to him. He spent his free time with us and loved playing with our boys. He was a senior high school student from the province center of Tam Ky—south on Route One about halfway to Quang Ngai. He came to Danang for his schooling. When he told us his background, we were amazed. When in junior high, he walked home from school one day and he saw two American GIs on the street. Wanting to practice his English, he said to them, "Hello, how are you?" One of them replied with the conventional, "Fine, how are you?" Then the other said, "You speak good English. What religion are you?" Hien, a nominal Buddhist, had heard that few

Americans were Buddhist, so he thought about his history lessons and said, "I am Pilgrim." "Pilgrim?" they asked curiously. Sensing this was wrong he then said, "Oh, I mean I am Puritan." This seemed to further confuse them, so then he said, "I am Protestant." This they understood, so they commended the young boy and went on their way.

Hien had gone to the Buddhist pagoda quite frequently with his aunt, but he realized he really had no "religion." So, the next day he went to the Tin Lanh Church and saw a young girl playing in the churchyard. "Take me to your monk," he said. "We don't have monks," she answered. "Well, then take me to your priest." "We don't have priests either," she said. "Well, take me to whatever you have," he insisted. "We have my daddy," said the young girl, who happened to be the pastor's young daughter. She led him inside where he heard the good news of how to find peace with God for the first time. He prayed with the pastor and made the great transaction from death to eternal life and was "born again" according to Jesus' words in the Gospel of John. From then on he became active with the church youth and learned the Bible along with his other studies.

When we needed an interpreter, we used Hien. Over the next three years he endeared himself to many western speakers by his good humor, servant heart, and excellent English. Dr. Ravi Zacharias, the well-known Christian apologist, held meetings in Danang, and Hien did a good job interpreting for him. In fact, the two became friends and kept in contact with one another after the event. During our next four years in Danang, Hien became like a son to us and brother to our boys. We had dreams for his future, but things turned out very differently.

Hien's future would take strange turns. When he finished high school several years later, we secured a full scholarship for him at Nyack College in New York—our alma mater. But before he could take advantage of this, Hien was conscripted into the Vietnamese military "for the duration of the war." We were all crushed at this change of plans. His education and abilities admitted him to officer's training and he rose quickly in rank. About this time we would be finishing our four-year term in Danang and going home for our second furlough.

In 1975, when we were living in Penang, Malaysia, on what we thought would be a temporary two-year assignment, Vietnam fell to the Communists. As things disintegrated we knew Hien would be in big trouble due to his military involvement. We sent word to our missionaries still in Vietnam asking them to find him and get him out of the country. We promised to bear all expenses. No one could locate him. Over the next few years we used every contact we had to try to discover what had happened to him. News was scarce and slowly trickled out. Finally, a few years later we heard that he had tried to escape on one of the unseaworthy craft used by the "boat people" escapees during those years, but a huge, typhoon-like storm assailed his boat and all on board were lost at sea. We were devastated.

Imagine our shock two years later to receive word from a refugee camp in Indonesia that Hien was alive and safe. It was like a resurrection. Hien went on to be accepted for refugee resettlement in California, attend UC Berkeley, graduate with high honors, and find a job in the financial field. It wouldn't be until after his graduation in the late eighties that we finally met face to face with Hien. He came to New York to visit us and we took him to see Niagara Falls. On that trip we heard his amazing story.

Immediately after the fall of Vietnam to the Communists in 1975, Hien was arrested and taken to a re-education camp. He was incarcerated in a twenty-foot metal ship container with many other former military officers and given a space of about eighteen inches on the floor. Later he was transferred to a regional prison where their captors allowed them outside for shower privileges only once or twice a week. Otherwise, they were confined in their space. They were not allowed to speak in any language other than Vietnamese and they had absolutely no literature to read beside Communist propaganda. Loud broadcasts continued from dawn to dusk extolling the virtues of socialism and the teachings of Lenin, Marx, and the Vietnamese hero, Ho Chi Minh.

Each night Hien would lie face down on his pillow and recite Bible verses he had memorized, then he would pray asking for God's help and release from this place. After some time had passed he thought to himself, "I don't think God hears me; nothing seems to happen, maybe I have been deluded." As he listened to the constant brainwashing, he thought that perhaps socialism was right; that he was evolving into more understanding. Just maybe he was first a Buddhist, then had a higher thought and became a Christian, and now was being offered an even higher thought—to become a Communist. He decided to "test God." He would resist his habit of prayer and recalling Bible verses before bedtime and see if anything was different. It was not. So, he began to think, "If I pray, nothing happens. If I don't pray, nothing happens. So why pray? God, if there is one, is not listening."

One day, right about this time, he got the coveted assignment of cleaning the prison officers' latrines. This meant he could be outdoors more than usual and feel some sun on his skin. By now almost all the prisoners had severe skin problems due to lack of good nutrition and sunshine. Their meals consisted primarily of a thin soup and rice. That day as he was cleaning the latrines he saw some paper which had actually been used as toilet paper. As he picked it up he noticed that it had writing on it in English. Something to read! He wiped it off, tucked it into his shorts and went about his work. That night, he lay on his stomach and secretly pulled the paper from his pocket to read it.

What had he found? He had found a portion of scripture. And not just any scripture, but the beautiful passage in Romans 8 which says:

"Who shall separate us from the love of Christ? Shall trouble or hardship or persecution or famine or nakedness or danger or sword? . . . No, in all these things we are more than conquerors through him who loved us. For I am convinced that neither death nor life, neither angels nor demons, neither the present nor the future, nor any powers, neither height nor depth, nor anything else in all creation, will be able to separate us from the love of God that is in Christ Jesus our Lord." (vs 35, 37-39).

Hien understood immediately that God had given him this personal message in this remarkable way as an answer to his prayers. He did not doubt again.

A few days after this, an officer called Hien into the camp office quite roughly. Once inside, the camp commander offered him a soft drink from his own rations and said, "I have noticed something different about you. I will put you on the release list. But publicly I still must treat you the same as others, and not tell them I have done this for you." Then he sent him out of the office. Within a few months Hien was released.

Some months later, Hien, made clandestine plans to escape on a fishing boat with thirty-eight others. Just as they approached the international water boundary line, a Vietnamese government patrol boat opened fire on their boat. Hien surrendered and sank his fishing boat. He was arrested and thrown into prison again. He was heartsick but did not lose faith in God. This is why we had heard the news he had been lost at sea.

After his release, Hien moved to the Mekong Delta and met an influential woman who helped him register and build a tugboat, which he used to haul gravel to construction sites at the mouth of the Mekong River. After some time, having established himself well, he made a plan to escape on one of his trips to the river mouth. He had over fifty people who were going with him and on the chosen night, they made a rendezvous at one of the river towns.

Just as all of them had boarded and were about to leave, three members of the shore patrol appeared with guns trained on the tugboat. "Halt!" they called. "What are you doing?" Hien explained that he was taking grains to the larger ship and showed them his license. "Then who are these people on the boat with you?" they questioned. "Oh, they are going home from market and are used to catching a ride with me to the next town," was Hien's offhand reply.

"Stop!" the men insisted. "Are you trying to escape Vietnam?" Hien realized that he was lying and threw himself on their mercy. "Please," he said. "Yes, we are trying to escape. Please let us go." Back came the astonishing reply, "We want to go with you!" Two of the men got on board and the third disappeared into the town: the boat went downriver and out to sea—another miracle in the life of Hien. When they got into the open sea a big storm blew up, the night was black, and it was impossible to navigate by a compass or the stars. The two well-trained naval men were able to navigate the ship safely to Indonesia, where the refugees were taken to a camp. From there Hien and his two brothers were eventually sent to the United States.

Today Hien lives in southern California and it is a joy for us to periodically see him and his wife and family, and to reminisce about the two angels God planted in the Vietnamese shore patrol one dark and stormy night.

Ravi Zacharias preaches

CHAPTER SEVENTEEN

Hiên interprets

CHAPTER 18

SAM STEMPLE

Our second son, Sam, was born during our furlough in Ohio. He was nine months old and beginning to crawl everywhere as we prepared to return to Vietnam. At our request, our pediatrician gave us a one-time dose of Phenobarbitol to give Sam on the long 16-hour trip from the U.S. west coast to Saigon. Since he was under two years of age, we did not have to buy him a ticket, but we did have to hold him the entire trip.

Unknown to us, Sam is one of the small percentage of people who react in exactly the opposite way as intended from that medication. Soon after we got on the plane, he began to bounce instead of nod off. Then his face turned red, his eyes got bright and I am sure his hairs stood on end. He would not calm down and kept poking people and saying "Hi," to them, smiling and singing, or trying to get off the seat and crawl. The Cathay Pacific flight attendants volunteered to hold him whenever they could, but we had to keep following him up and down the aisle to prevent him from crawling under the seats or bumping other sleeping travelers the entire time. That trip defined much of Sam's young life—active, happy, friendly and often doing the unexpected. He took that to Vietnam and seemed to adjust very easily.

His brother, Stewart, was three and a half when we returned and he easily slipped right back into his Vietnamese language and culture. He fit the role of Sam's wonderful big brother: adviser, teacher, leader, roommate, playmate, and sometimes bully. Each year Grandma Stemple would send Easter clothes for the boys to wear complete with ties, dress shirts, and new pants. We marked the years by those photos which today bring hilarious laughter from them both.

The boys became familiar with the big Danang neighborhood; they played with the Vietnamese children and were often out by the market. Chi Lien, Sam's occasional babysitter, would take him out to the market when she bought her breakfast soup, which was spicy hot. We would tell her, "Don't give Sam any of that soup," and she would vow not to do it. But each time she came back carrying Sam, we would see the telltale red marks around his lips and we knew he had begged for, and gotten, some of her soup. Today his favorite foods are still hot and hotter and he adds chilies to anything and everything. You just can't see the red marks as well.

We frequently got the boys haircuts from the local barber, who had a traveling business. We would hear him coming down the street hitting two sticks together, signaling his trade. We would go out with the boys and tell him they needed their hair cut, and he would be so pleased as they were good advertisement for him. He would begin by unfolding his tin traveling table with the shelves on the side and mirror at the back. Next would come his folding "camp stool" for the client. From his pockets he would produce the straight razor, strop, hand clippers, and various other tools of his trade, including his duster, pomades, and creams.

Stewart usually went first with his luxurious curly brown hair. "Oh look," the barber would call, "Come and see. I have an American child here. Come look at this duck-tail." People would gather around and see how Stewart's hair came to a natural duck-tail in the back. Stewart would sit there and smile precociously as the people would say, *Ngoan qua,* meaning, "he is well-behaved and will grow up to be very clever or wise."

I had to "stand guard" for both boys and emphasize that all I wanted was a haircut. The barber would argue that I would not get my money's worth; the price for the haircut (about twenty cents) covered much more than just cutting hair. It included: reaming out the wax in the ear with a dainty, thin, spoon-shaped, small gold tool; cutting the nose hairs; cracking the neck with a real adjustment; adding pomade to the hair and slicking it back; and finally, liberally sprinkling "toilet water" over the face and neck of the happy customer. Everyone knew who had just been to the barber so he was unwilling to let my boys go without the works; it would hurt his reputation. But I stood firm on everything except the toilet water.

After Stewart, Sam would have his turn and he could barely wait. He got up on the stool and grinned from ear to ear as the barber called out again, "Come look at this American head. You have never seen anything like it. Here are two whirlpools!" Poor Sam had two big cowlicks; one on each side of the top of his head, somewhat like Dagwood Bumstead of the comics. They made cutting his hair almost impossible. Embarrassed? No, not Sam, who played king of the neighborhood with all the attention. As the people would come and look, they would shake their heads and say, "*Oh, nghich qua, nghich qua*" This means, he is really mischievous. The funny thing is, Stewart is now a businessman and Sam works with youth. Maybe, just maybe, there is something about ducktails and cowlicks that we are just too sophisticated to catch!

We spent a lot of time reading to the boys and playing simple games. The favorite for Sam was the board game *Sorry.* Before he knew how to say his numbers or read a word, he knew which card meant "go backward," which card would start a play, and above all, which card he could grab out, hold up triumphantly and yell, "Sorry!" We got into a routine each evening of having our prayers together and then playing a round of *Sorry* before the boys went to bed.

About that time we took a vacation to the mountain town of Dalat. It was once a resort town for the French colonials, and also the former site of the American boarding school for the children of Vietnamese missionaries. The city was modern, the weather was cool, the flowers and vegetables beautiful and plentiful, and it remained about the only good, safe place for a vacation. The actual school had been moved out of the country due to the war so the former dorms were available for vacation rooms at a reasonable cost.

We bought our tickets on Air Vietnam and flew from Danang to Dalat after more than two years of intense ministry. The Dalat airport is about 20 kilometers from the town. We were enjoying the bus ride through the colorful jungle areas when our bus was suddenly halted. The Viet Cong had blown up the bus ahead of us killing all on board, not to mention completely destroying the road making it impassable. We got off the bus with our luggage and sat by the side of the road; unable to go back where we had come from, but not sure we wanted to go ahead either. We waited for the road to be cleared and for another bus to come from the far side to transport us. We would need to walk across the devastated area to the other bus when it got there.

As we patiently sat by the road with our fellow passengers, we were all grateful we had not been on that first bus. Suddenly Sam looked at me and said, "Mommy, did you bring the *Sorry*?" Yes, it was in the suitcase. We pulled out the board, the deck of cards, and the little plastic bag of parts including the dice and spread it all out by the side of the road. For the next hour, we played *Sorry* and had a little island of "normal" in a frightful time and place. I guess "home" is not necessarily a place, but a feeling of refuge and rightness and of being with those you love. They eventually cleared the road and we got to Dalat for a wonderful week's vacation.

Everyone in the family took worm medicine; Sam was a "good host." He had roundworms and frequently they out-witted the medication. We had bouts of head lice, but knew what to do with those; the short haircuts helped the most. Sam was usually healthy, both on the outside and inside, in spite of eating everything in sight. But one period of time, when our city's population doubled from war and refugees, the pollution caused him to get a terrible skin infection called "muc" by the Vietnamese. Small, purulent blisters were all over his face, and became exacerbated by his constant perspiring and then wiping his face with his dirty hands. I washed him daily with Phisohex soap (although banned in American pharmacies) and he screamed as I touched him. No matter how hard I tried to isolate him—within minutes he was dirty again.

Soon Sam's face became one swollen, infected mess. It looked like a pitted pumpkin. We got scared. I took him to an American doctor who told me the only way to get rid of this was to get him into a clean sterile air-conditioned environment until it healed. Where on earth would that be?

At this same time Woody and I were both working furiously in refugee ministries and busy each day. But I decided that I would drop everything, fly with Sam to Saigon and stay in our guest home's air conditioned rooms until he healed. Then we prayed for him. The next day we began to make arrangements but noticed Sam seemed a bit better. By the end of a week, Sam's face was clear as a bell and he had no scarring. You would think we would have known to pray first! We thanked God and also thanked the many people praying for us so faithfully. And I don't think he ever did get teen-age acne!

Sam spent all of his preschool days in Danang. He learned the language, had lots of Vietnamese and missionary-kid friends, loved the food, and enjoyed going to the children's classes at the church next door. He mimicked Stewart in every action, which drove Stewart nuts. Every day we would hear, "Mom, make him stop copying me." The idea that imitation was the sincerest form of flattery did not impress Stewart, but he was a good (if impatient) brother to Sam. He just refused to order food in a restaurant before Sam, because he did NOT want Sam copying him again. Sam's hardest time was when Stewart left for school, but Sam was not alone in that.

Sam traveled all over with us, except to the refugee camps. We have pictures of him in his treehouse, in the children's choir, and with his brother. My favorite one is of him on beautiful China Beach standing in the surf with his arms crossed like the king of his world. As incongruous as it sounds, Sam had a happy, normal childhood surrounded by love and adventure, and he never knew he was in the midst of a historical war "up close and personal."

CHAPTER EIGHTEEN

Shelly Josephsen SAm Rob Drummond
August 1970

Chi Lien

Sam's mucs

CHAPTER 19

NURSE GWEN

O ne day some U.S. Marine officers came to our house in Danang to visit me. They told me that they had built a pediatric hospital on the outskirts of the city in an area called Hoa Khanh and they needed my help. They had hired thirty-five young women as "nurses" from the neighborhood, and were giving them on-the-job training in caring for the children, but they needed some better professional training. Since I am a registered nurse, they asked me to come once a week to teach these girls fundamentals of nursing. This would be a volunteer job.

I did not want to do this; I did not have the time and I did not want to dig out my nursing books and translate the materials; the preparation would be difficult. But they persuaded me, and I agreed. Within a week I took a Lambro out to the Hoa Khanh area with folders in hand to teach basic nursing skills as elementary as TPR (temperature, pulse, and respiration). I also had to impart the culturally different idea of nurse as custodial care giver; not only pill dispenser and dressing changer.

One of the first people I met was the "head nurse," Nguyen Thi Khang. Her Vietnamese name was too difficult for Americans to pronounce, so everybody called her

Nurse Gwen. I had already heard about her; she was a major celebrity in Danang. As I learned her story, partly from her and partly from the American personnel, I found out that she had been a big part of raising funds for this beautiful, state-of-the-art facility complete with about 120 beds and all the necessary departments—lab, surgery, dietary, radiology, and pharmacy. It seems that Gwen was originally a seamstress in Danang and when the Americans came in big numbers, she moved her shop out by the base to sew souvenir clothing and gifts for the GIs to purchase. After a while, she noticed that the men in the medical unit, on their free time went out into the villages to care for sick children. This intrigued her and she began volunteering to go along.

Gwen quickly picked up English and became an invaluable help in working with the children. The need had become so great that the men began to bring children to a central area to be cared for and eventually established a sort of tent hospital. They named Gwen the "Head Nurse." When they conceived the dream of building a lasting hospital, the military doctors took Gwen with them to the United States to raise funds. Military officers in private helicopters escorted her from place to place, gave her special VIP treatment, and took her to meet President Nixon. A large picture of him shaking her hand hung in the hospital and her home. The mayor of Los Angeles declared "Nurse Gwen Day," and my hometown of Akron, Ohio gave her the keys to the city, as did several other cities. She stayed in private homes and met many people. The trip was successful and the hospital was built. Gwen was now the official head nurse.

Nurse Gwen had become quite famous for her "plastic surgery." Many of the children who came to the hospital were burn victims and often needed large areas of skin grafted. Gwen would use the dermatome to take micro-thin layers of skin from the buttocks or hips, cut a pattern and place this good skin over the burned area, then stitch it carefully in place with tiny silk stitches. Remember, she had been a seamstress. Sometimes she used the pink paper tape (used in my day to set curls along the face) to hold the skin in place. In either case, she had very little or no scarring. The American plastic surgeons liked to watch her work.

This reminds me that studies have shown that Vietnamese in general have the best "small motor skills" of almost any people group. This explains why they do such beautiful embroidery, are much in demand for factory work on computer chips, and have "cornered" the nail business in the United States. They can hold their thumbs opposed to their index finger for long periods of time while working on miniscule projects with fine detail.

Nurse Gwen and I bonded quickly. Soon after I began teaching the nurses, I asked her if she was interested in doing a one-on-one Bible study with me. To my shock, she threw her arms around me and said, "This is what I have been waiting for. When I was in the United States, I stayed with a host family who introduced me to Jesus Christ, but I need to know more. I am afraid to go to the church because I don't know what they do in there." Then she told me she wanted to study with me every night of the week. Well, I have never had such an eager response, but I settled with her for Monday evenings only; and for the next few years she grew in her Christian faith by leaps and bounds as she studied, memorized and applied God's Word to her life.

Meanwhile, our nursing classes continued. One day, Gwen challenged me, "You should be ashamed of yourself," she said. "You come here to teach nursing but they need to know the Bible, too. You should come twice a week to teach Bible." "Well," I sputtered back, "the Marines invited me to teach nursing." "I'm the head nurse, and I say what the nurses learn." This was the final word, and from then on I went twice a week for Bible. All thirty-five of those girls responded so positively to the teaching of scripture and a relationship with Jesus; and today I still follow many of their lives, including some who married pastors.

After the American military left, the hospital was turned over completely to the World Relief Commission, and American doctors and nurses staffed it very competently, along with their Vietnamese co-workers, until the end of the war. Again, Gwen found herself rising to the task of Head Nurse and everyone who came there appreciated her greatly. She had three children and adopted one more Amerasian child, named Scotty, whom we all loved dearly.

When South Vietnam fell to the Communists in 1975, Woody and I were already on assignment in Penang, Malaysia. During those hectic final days in Danang, when people were hanging on to the skids of helicopters to escape, Nurse Gwen tried desperately to evacuate with her family to safety. She had been so intimately involved with Americans that she would be in great danger after the takeover. Word finally arrived from San Jose, California, that Gwen had escaped through the refugee channels but her family had not. Cheerfully she wrote me that God had given her five years to learn English and nursing, five years to study the Bible with me, and within five years she believed she would be reunited with her family. That was in 1975.

In 1980 the first of her family arrived in the States and today they are all well settled in California. She worked for many years in the San Jose medical system, became a leader in the local Vietnamese church and raised her children. Now she is retired, in shaky health due to severe allergies, but still enjoying her church and her grandchildren. I have visited her many times in her home where we talk and catch up and where her husband makes me my wonderful, strong, filtered-in-the-cup Vietnamese morning coffee laced with sweetened condensed milk. I speak at her church, or at a women's gathering, or just "hang out" with a wonderful woman whose life has influenced hundreds of people. She could well live in the past with her great memories and moments of fame, but she is still excited about learning and obeying what God is showing her each day. Her prayer life and inner life are alive and full, and her memories always lead her to the present she enjoys and the future she anticipates. My own experience is so much richer because God and the Marines brought Nurse Gwen into my life.

CHAPTER NINETEEN

Gwen meets President Nixon

CHAPTER 20

TRAVELS AND TENSIONS

Within a year of our arrival in Danang there was no doubt that tensions were escalating. We could tune into the local military frequency and actually hear where the incoming cannon rounds were expected to land. The Danang airport was reportedly the busiest in the world; planes took off or landed every 30 seconds almost around the clock. Pastors and people came in from the countryside telling of troop buildups in their areas.

At one point a country church called *Chien Dang* invited us to be the guest speakers at a big evening meeting. It was the first time we had been anywhere near there after dark, but the pastor was a dear friend and he told us it would be okay. During the meeting, tanks rolled through the neighborhood and a full-scale battle ensued. I clearly remember trying to complete a lesson on Daniel and feeling like we, ourselves, were in the "lion's den." We got home safely but the pastor apologized about the extra thrills of that night.

By now five more new missionaries had arrived and were in language study. Part of our job was to oversee their studies, give periodic tests, and help them get acquainted with life in Vietnam. The Johnsons with two teen-age children, and three single women got started with their tutors. They definitely raised the level of excitement in the neighborhood. All but one would eventually be assigned to work with ethnic minorities, but meanwhile, Vietnamese study remained their first priority. They helped out tremendously in our country church and other military ministries.

Over the next two years our lives became a blur of activity in spite of the tensions. In addition to Vietnam's military conflict, internal politics simmered to the boiling point. One Sunday we got out of Church as the smell and smoke of burning rubber filled the air. We were told to get home and into the house, so we did. Almost immediately shooting started in the streets; a real skirmish between the Buddhists and the local police broke out. A new edict had come out stating that the Buddhist flag had to be lower than the government flag which enraged and mobilized the Buddhists. Now a "new battle" was distracting government troops. Piles of burning tires lined all four sides of the intersection on the corner where we lived. A firefight broke out—shooting and shouting filled the air. At one point, almost simultaneously, a shot was fired, a thud was heard, Norm Johnson fell to the floor, and something shattered. We immediately thought Norm had been hit by gunfire. A quick examination showed that Norm had heard the shot, fell to the floor as we all did, and hit the bookcase where a vase was located thus shattering it. We sat scattered on the floor nervously laughing as we realized the dark humor of the situation. Woody later glued the vase back together and it stands as another reminder in our home of God's protection.

A short time after that the Tin Lanh church in the village of Phu Phong in Qui Nhon province invited us to special meetings. We flew to the province center of Qui Nhon as a family and were hosted by veteran missionaries, Mr. and Mrs. Chester Travis. Our four rode in the back seat as Mr. Travis drove his car to the country church, giving us quite a memorable ride. His vehicle was known all over the province because he had a PA system hooked on to the roof and all the way along he played on his harmonica as he drove. In each market town along the way we would stop while he drew a crowd and then he gave the gospel message. The people loved and respected him because of his age; this beloved couple had lived in Qui Nhon longer than most of them and everyone knew them. Their white hair and their obvious love of the people erased any thought of the strangeness of their methods.

I remember that it was very hot as we rode along with all the car windows open. Mrs. Travis regularly threw Gospel tracts out the window as we rode, so a crowd of people followed behind picking them up. Because of the car and wind speed, lots of the tracts flew right back into the back seat, but I hadn't noticed. Our longsuffering, four-year-old Stewart finally asked, "Mommy, why does Auntie Travis keep throwing papers at me? Please ask her to stop." There on his lap were a good stack of airborne missiles intended for the masses.

The church meeting went well, but became overshadowed by our memorable trip back to Qui Nhon. The old car lost all gears but reverse, so we backed down the highway, with the PA system blaring, the harmonica playing, Uncle Travis steering with one hand, and people and animals scattering in our wake. We made it safely back. The two boys thought it was a wonderful adventure, but we felt very good to fly back to Danang and a bit more normal life, although that would be a matter of perspective. Ours would not be considered normal by most standards.

The fighting was erratic and sporadic; sometimes one area would be very dangerous; other times it would be peaceful. There were times that the Josephsen family, who lived north of us in the former Imperial Capital of Hue, would need to cross the Hai Van Pass and come down to stay in Danang for a period. Even more often, the Drummond family in

Quang Ngai, our former home, would have to come north for a period of time. We all relied mainly on our pastors and people to tell us when to come and go, but we also listened to military advice and were under the direction of the U.S. Embassy in the long run. Although the times were tense and it was difficult to live temporarily with others, it was always fun to have the fellowship and help; after all everyone knew Vietnamese and could "plug in" anywhere. Sometimes these colleagues stayed with us for a week; sometimes a month. This is when I was most thankful for a cook and house help!

At one period of time when the Drummond family had "evacuated" Quang Ngai and had come to Danang, they were living in one of the empty language student apartments. It was rainy season and we could see that a big storm was brewing. They came to our house for a meal and while we were together a huge wind blew up and came at high speed through our property. We all hunkered down in our house as we heard the sound of trees crashing down, branches snapping, windows and tiles breaking, and people hollering. It was a typhoon. When the worst had passed the Drummonds went over to their house to find trees had fallen on it and crashed right through to the bedroom they would have been in. Blue tarps had to be stretched over the holes. It took weeks to clean up the debris and repair the damages, but thankfully, no adults or children were included in that account.

At another point the Drummond family had been with us about a month and were told it was safe to return to Quang Ngai. In many ways it was a relief to be a "nuclear family" again, but that night I dreamed that they returned. I laughingly told Woody I must have been under more tension than I realized. We sat eating breakfast when a knock came on the door. The Drummond family was back. Beth was crying; she felt so bad that they were back on our doorstep. It seemed that they had no sooner returned to Quang Ngai than big fighting broke out and the pastors told them to get out of town again. I assured her that God had warned me and that I was waiting. Neither one of us could believe it, but we were together again and this would not be the last time .

Thievery was rampant all over Vietnam but especially in Danang. Stealing from Americans became a kind of "Robin Hood" mentality—they have the goods and they are rich—we don't and we are poor; we can right this wrong. Personally, we were very careful whenever we left our house. We held tight or hid purses, cameras and items of importance. We knew literally hundreds of stories of loss by thieves. One ploy was for two guys on a motorbike to drive by Americans in a cyclo or with their arms resting on their open truck or car window. The driver would swerve toward the vehicle and the guy in back would give a mighty slap and grab at the wrist-watch, which typically had an expandable band. Off they would speed before you knew what hit you. Woody prided himself in avoiding thieves. He had his watchband broken, but never lost a watch. I, on the other hand, was holding Stewart one day when a crowd of women gathered around me to "ooh and ahh" at my beautiful baby and ask to hold him. I proudly showed him off and when they left, my watch was gone too. Diversion was their successful tactic.

One of our missionaries went to Saigon to get the Danang mission monthly payment; quite a large amount of money that had to be hand carried since there was no bank transfer. He was carrying it in a briefcase down a main Saigon avenue when a girl accosted him and began rubbing his legs. He tried to push her away but she persisted. Distracted, he did not notice her accomplice until she grabbed his briefcase and ran off with the money. We would have teased him more about that if it hadn't been such an expensive loss.

Visitors came from Saigon one day to photograph some of our ministry. They had very good cameras so Woody warned them to guard them at all times. We stopped at one of our churches to pray for a sick pastor's wife and one man left his camera in the van. As they bowed their heads to pray in the parsonage, Woody "watched and prayed" and saw someone get into the van and grab the camera and begin to run. Woody raced from the house and down the street after the young kid and all the neighbors came out to watch the contest. When Woody caught the young man, he had no camera; he had ditched it. Noticing that one bystander had glanced at a pile of trash alongside the road, Woody went to the pile and kicked it. There was a telltale camera strap, and the missing camera was recovered. The people were impressed.

In that same area lots of American military convoys roared constantly between the airfield and the bases. Huge trucks filled with goods would rumble down the road with soldiers on top of the loads guarding them. The local gangs figured out a successful way to steal from these soft-hearted Americans. One of them would get a cane and fake a limp and cross the street in front of the truck, which would always slow down and then stop when the kid fell down. Immediately lots more kids would converge on the truck from both sides of the road and strip it bare. How could they shoot those kids? It was a never-ending problem.

A chaplain came to visit us and as Woody went outside with him to his Jeep, he saw a young boy working on the rear-view mirror to remove it. Just as he got it loose, Woody grabbed him, pinioned his arms, and took his screwdriver. He wailed, howled and kicked until Woody put him down and he ran off. That night our telephone rang. No one ever called us; it was seldom a functional phone. When I answered I heard a Vietnamese voice roughly talking to me and threatening us. I was not sure what he was saying, so I finally put down the phone, thinking it was a wrong number. I told Woody that someone was telling me that the man with the screwdriver is going to get his house bombed tonight. What in the world is he talking about? Imagine how I felt when

Woody held up the offending screwdriver and asked, "This one?" Thankfully, it was just a threat.

Rick Drummond had an International Carryall vehicle. One night while it was parked in our driveway, someone stole the wraparound windshield. Rick was very upset but able to get a replacement from the U.S. Army motor pool. A few days later he went out to find the second one stolen. This time he had to purchase a replacement. He cleverly welded "fingers" all around the windshield to protect it from theft. When he was driving a few weeks later he suddenly realized there was no glass in his window—just metal fingers around the edges. Someone had gotten it out without a problem. Rick solved the situation. He got one final windshield and this time he welded bars on it, inside and out. It felt like you were looking out of a jail cell, but last he knew, the window was still intact.

One afternoon I was in the back yard when I noticed that the big blue Air Force bus, which always dropped employees off at our corner, had pulled up on the side street next to our yard. I walked to the fence and watched as the driver welcomed about eight men with jerry-cans who came to stand by his gas tank. One by one they siphoned gas from the bus. When the line was almost finished the driver suddenly saw me standing watching the procedure. He hollered at the men who instantly scattered and then he came to me to try to explain in broken English that "they" made him do it. I began a long lecture in Vietnamese on Confucian morality and the breakdown in Vietnamese society while he stood open-mouthed listening to me lecture in his own language. Then he told me how poor he was, how this was the first time it had happened, how he would pay back the Air Force, and crying and imploring me for the sake of his starving wife and children to let him go. I told him I would report the incident but not tell the Americans who it was and where it happened.

He gratefully drove away and I didn't see it happen again — that is, not on my corner.

We did take time off as a family, usually about once a week. We would go visit with friends in town or we would go out to eat at one of the local restaurants especially enjoying lobster or giant prawns right from the sea. The famed China Beach was nearby and a group of us often went there to swim, although sharing the beach with lots of military men on R&R was a bit daunting. They would always come up and inspect our families who seemed so out of place there, and they were always surprised to learn there were missionaries in Danang. One guy felt sure we had said "mercenaries" and gave us quite a lecture. Several times a year, and almost every Fourth of July, we took our favorite outing. We would go with the Stan Smith family on their mission launch out to the private beach where they had a leprosarium. Although this beach was part of the greater Danang harbor, and just under the Hai Van Pass to Hue, it could only be reached by water and was very isolated. We brought the fixings for a cookout and spent the whole day there. The water was crystal clear and the cares of Danang, let alone the whole world, seemed as remote as the beach. Passing the huge U.S. Navy warships at anchor as we returned at the end of the day brought us back to reality

Customarily, the country churches held a "Short-term Bible School" (STBS) during the rice farming off-season just after the harvest. It was a kind of discipleship training for teen-agers and adults, both men and women. Usually lasting two weeks, the participants would come and live at the church — eating, fellowshipping, and learning together. One year Woody and I were invited to teach at a STBS in Tam Ky, the province center between Danang and Quang Ngai. Woody went the first week and I went the second. My topic was the life and lessons from the account of Elijah and Elisha as recorded in the book of Kings. I studied hard, preparing the best I could for these multi-generational lessons. The best part of the week was living together with the women students; bathing at the well, using the outdoor facilities, sleeping in one of the Sunday School classrooms on a wooden bed without a mattress, using the mosquito nets, sharing in simple meals, and feeling the rhythms of life in the countryside. I sat in on other classes and at the end of the week all my students passed my course.

But when I went to go north to Danang we learned the road had been cut, and my only option for getting home was by helicopter. One of the students took me on the back of his motor bike to the landing strip. I sat on an old straw cart there, unable to communicate with anyone about my situation, and hoping that the daily helicopter pick-up would indeed show up. I could not see a human being the entire time I waited there, but I was more worried about the ones who were probably watching me from an unseen spot. The helicopter came, totally shocked to see a lone American woman waiting for a ride. I got home safely with great memories from my first and only STBS. Unbelievably, when my good friend, Pastor Minh Dang in Akron, and I got reacquainted thirty years later, we realized he was a young student of mine in that class. He even claims he remembers the lessons.

For a few months about mid-term we had a wonderful temporary change in ministry. The pastor and family at the Saigon International Church had completed their time and there would be a three-month hiatus until the next pastor arrived. They asked Woody to "fill in" as the interim pastor and so we moved temporarily to the lovely, spacious second floor apartment of the building adjacent to the church building in the lovely tree-lined district of Saigon quite close to the palace and U.S. embassy.

The first floor of the large L-shaped building housed the U.S. Servicemen's Center which doubled as church classrooms; the second floor was the tall church sanctuary which actually was two stories high. The pastor's apartment was on second floor, and another missionary family had the third floor of the L-shaped building. Woody really enjoyed preaching in English and we loved the large congregation composed of military, diplomatic, and business people who temporarily made Saigon their home. I remember that one of the first things we did when we arrived was to follow the new order from the U.S. embassy to crisscross all our large glass windows with tape in case of explosions. It didn't quite look like stained glass, but the worship together in those strained circumstances was awesome.

The new pastor came and we happily went back to Danang, but then another temporary assignment came which would end up changing our lives as well as the course of the church in Vietnam. Woody was asked to go to the coastal city of Nhatrang to teach a modular course on apologetics to the students at the Bible School/Seminary. He would teach concentrated classes for two weeks using a Vietnamese interpreter. Again, we went as a family and Woody studied up and prepared diligently. We were to stay in the home of Professor Orrel and Gini Steinkamp, our good friends and mentors from our language study days in Danang. It would be a vacation for the boys and me. We all flew down in great anticipation.

The very evening we arrived, Orrel did not arrive home as expected from his class. As the evening progressed we received word that a spiritual awakening or revival had broken out and students were praying, weeping, and calling for God to empower them. We all went to bed and in the morning discovered what had happened. As Orrel was teaching on the great revivals of the church throughout history, many of the students wanted to know why it could not happen again in their lives and church. As they began to weep and confess their sin before God, and plead for Him to help the Vietnamese church in its hour of need, the presence of God became almost palpable. This overcoming feeling of God's presence and love stayed with the class for over a week: classes were suspended, restitutions were made, apologies given, and a great new refreshing came to the students and faculty. Woody completed his classes and we returned home to Danang thrilled about the experience the students had had.

The revival spirit continued and as the students went home for Christmas break they continued to teach about God's power to bring joy and love into situations and whole churches experienced great changes. This produced a new vitality and urgency in the churches. Then when the missionaries met in Saigon at conference, we experienced a wonderful time of brokenness, deepening, and renewing of spiritual life through the biblical preaching, teaching and prayer. Many of us, Woody and I included, came to conference physically exhausted and spiritually dry. Almost everyone went home energized by God's spirit in ways too sacred and personal to even write about. I myself know it happened to me. In fact, on a bus in Saigon as I was pondering the work of the Holy Spirit and the gifts He gives individuals, I know He gave me an overpowering gift of love. This extended to people I knew and did not know—in Vietnam, America, and around the world—and has been the hallmark of my life since that time. We called it Revival! Since then, as we look back at that spiritual highlight we believe God strengthened both the missionaries and the Vietnamese church for what was to come. Only God's hand on lives and deep personal faith could have kept the church through the dark days that lay ahead.

I had been invited by the Vietnamese women's organization to speak to a district women's conference in the province center of Qui Nhon. Due to reports of a deteriorating situation there, I wavered about going. I sent a telegram to Mr. and Mrs. Travis to get their opinion, but received no answer.

The ladies insisted I go and that things were fine, so I flew down. I was met with a military jeep driven by a Vietnamese colonel whose wife was one of the organizers. She and two other women were so excited to welcome me and give me the plans for the weekend. They insisted on honking the horn all the way into town. On the way to the place we were all staying they asked if I wanted to stop and pay a formal visit on the Travises. Of course I said yes.

When we pulled into the Travis home, they were astonished. "What are you doing here?" they wanted to know. "We sent you a telegram not to come; things are very tense here." When they learned I had not gotten the telegram they advised me to turn around and go home. The women and the colonel said it would not be necessary. When the Travises insisted I stay with them instead of with the Vietnamese organizers, the ladies capitulated, and the Travises promised they would have me at the church for all the meetings as scheduled.

When I went into their house, it was unbelievable. Chester, ever the "inventor," had rigged up an alarm system that consisted of wires everywhere, all attached to doors. There were lids, pans, metal pieces, and all kinds of noisemakers roped together, so that if any door opened, it tripped the wires. I hung my dress on a wire in what I thought was the closet in the little bedroom they gave me: it set off a string of banging objects all the way to the kitchen including bells and whistles. Later as I went to sleep, the radio kept coming on and off, as did some lights, at odd erratic hours all night long. They wanted to prove to any intruders that they were awake, alert and on guard.

They apologized for not having anything for me to eat except eggs; I was happy for a supper of scrambled eggs and French bread. Then I found out that they had a "deal" with the local U.S. military; they collected the "leftovers" every day from the mess hall at the small base there. They fed these "slops" to their chickens, of which they had many. Then they sold the eggs for income. What they didn't sell, they ate; what they didn't eat, they put in the freezer. I opened the freezer for ice cubes only to see literally dozens of eggs stacked there all neatly dated on the shell with a magic marker. In spite of these eccentricities, Mr. and Mrs. Travis were dearly loved and respected for giving their lives and love to Vietnam—and they got me to church on time.

The second day as I spoke, our meeting was interrupted by a woman running into the service calling out "Our pastor has been captured. Our pastor has been captured." The Viet Cong had come in to a small town and taken the pastor away. All the women began to pray; not only for the pastor and his safety, but for wisdom on whether to continue the retreat. They felt they needed the teaching and we had only a half day to go to complete the schedule.

Back at the house before we went to bed, Chester and Mary got out a tape recording their grown children had made for them the past Christmas. It was full of singing, greetings from all their grandchildren, and obvious love and sentiment for the holiday. They told me of their loneliness at times and admitted they were glad I had come to bring some life and light into their lives. They were way past retirement age, but still felt they were needed by God and the Vietnamese church in Qui Nhon province.

That night, gunfire broke out very near to the Travis home and they called me to come quickly into the bathroom, the only "inside" room. There we sat huddled on the floor leaning against the bathtub the rest of the night as mortar rounds fell very near. We sang and prayed together; held hands and talked about our families and our journey with God until daybreak when quiet returned. That day I finished the retreat, said good-bye to Chester and Mary, and flew safely home to Danang. I left with a profound love and appreciation for my colleagues, and also for the courageous Vietnamese women who hungered to live for God in that land.

About a year later, the mission chairman came and literally packed up the Travis home and belongings and got them on a ship headed for retirement in California with their family. Mary insisted that her rocking chair be on deck so that she could enjoy the trip with the comforts of home. They represented a retired and dying "breed" of intrepid early missionaries who loved and learned and led the forming church of Vietnam. And as for me, there was almost never a week that passed that someone did not come by my house and tell me they had been at that Qui Nhon women's retreat and that God had spoken to them. There is no better way to live than making a difference in someone else's life, by the grace of God. And we knew we were safer in Vietnam in the center of God's will than anywhere else outside of it.

CHAPTER 20

SAIGON
INTERNATIONAL
CHURCH

planeload of noodles

Pastor Đô

Steinkamp Family

Mary + Chester Travis

Baptism
at
Chiên
Đàn

Tam Ky
Thầy
Tin

Short-term Bible School
Tam Ky

the typhoon
hits our
property

CHAPTER 21

MOVIE MAKERS

It was early January, 1972, and we had just come through a very busy Christmas season. We received a strange request from our field chairman in Saigon. He said we were to help Mr. Ken Anderson, a well-known Christian film maker who was coming from the United States to make an evangelistic film in Danang. This film would be done totally in the Vietnamese language and with Vietnamese personnel. Our part would be to host the three-member U.S. crew and the four main actors, find the "extras" for each scene, and prepare the sets for each day's shooting. We couldn't believe it, and we were a bit upset that such an incursion would be made on our schedule without prior warning or request. Nothing in our "normal" missionary training had prepared us for anything like this.

Within a week Mr. Anderson arrived with an assistant who did the sound, a photographer who did all the camera work, and four Vietnamese who would be the "main cast" of the movie—two young men and two young women. Our first tasks were to house and feed these friends, read the script, and learn what we were to do. Supposedly, we were to dedicate the following three weeks to this task.

Ken Anderson was a wonderful, genial professional with a gift of making the impossible possible! His vision was to make a Vietnamese film about the war which could be used in military hospitals, schools, and public theatres and clearly present the gospel. The story centered around a young Vietnamese man who was injured in the war and met a Christian nurse in the hospital where he had received a copy of the Gospel of John. Through the testimony of the nurse and of a good pre-war friend, and by reading the Word of God, he became a believer. The film was named, "The Peacemaker," but the Vietnamese church felt it should be renamed, so the original Vietnamese version is called, "The Strength of Love," and only the English version retains the "Peacemaker" title.

Our job was to meet with Mr. A and his group each evening for decisions on what scenes should be shot the next day followed by hiring painters who painted the "staged room" during the night. We borrowed, made, or bought the furnishings we would need and found the "extras" from among the young people except when scenes were "questionable" and the pastor would not let the youth participate. In that case we relied on neighborhood would-be-actors! It was wild.

I remember when we had one night to make the "café" scene. We hired the painters to paint the walls hot pink; went to the local café and borrowed tables and chairs (for a small price); made a "bar" at the end of the room; put together a believable disco set; and had the café ready for filming at 8:00 a.m. when the cast arrived.

And then there was the "bombing scene" when we had to "blow up" our café and then have fires in the grass in our backyard with people running through the area in the dark with lots of screaming and drama. We had to first get permission from the Danang police so they knew what we were doing with all the firecrackers and noise. Then one of our young people drizzled gasoline around on the grass and set the fires. This was the only scene Americans were in; our sons, Stewart and Sam, had great fun running through the sporadic fires back and forth along with dozens of adults, teens, and children. Because it was dark, you only saw feet and legs running through the fire-lit grass and no one could tell the nationality.

Oh yes, Woody was in one scene also. He drove the Tin Lanh van for the scene where they went out on a country road and the van got stopped by the VC (Viet Cong). We had to request military approval and actually receive real guards in order to shoot the film so that no one would think it was a real VC car stop. We had authentic weapons and uniforms, but you cannot see the driver when you watch the film. And for the gambling and drinking scenes, as well as the cyclo drivers, we had to go outside our gate and call in people off the street. Everyone was willing to come and play a part, and the whole neighborhood thought it was a terrific diversion.

When Ken announced we would shoot all the "rain scenes" the next day, I asked what would happen if it did not rain, especially since it was not rainy season. He assured me it never really rains in movie rain scenes. Sure enough, the next day was beautiful and sunny. But we went outside and thoroughly wetted down the house front as well as the people in the scene. The actors ran through a door with wet umbrellas while Woody sat on the roof and poured water down from the roof onto them. Rainmaker missionary! It really does look like it is raining in the movie version!

We also got permission to shoot many scenes in the Vietnamese military hospital; we then had to reproduce one of those rooms in our "scene room" for the close-ups. Matching the gray-green paint took a whole night. Thankfully, the hospital loaned us the bed, IV cart, bed table, and IV solutions to make it authentic and the film goes from broad view to close up without ever being evident it was shot in two locations.

This went on for three hectic weeks; by night I supervised the scene changes; by day I supervised the finding, caring for, feeding, transporting, and general oversight of 10-30 people. The youth group scenes and Sunday services at the church were authentic, except for the added cast sitting among the congregation. Finally, Ken called it a "wrap" and they all left Danang, with the promise to have the finished product as soon as possible.

And so we waited. About eight months later we got the finished, edited product—entirely shot in the Vietnamese language. It arrived a few months after the "Easter invasion" of 1972, which had pushed thousands of refugees from the northern provinces down into Danang and environs making a ready and receptive audience for this evangelistic film. The U.S. military had withdrawn and their empty camps were filled to overflowing with refugees (the U.S. base which held 4,000 U.S. marines now held 35,000 Vietnamese). Five months later, situations had been stabilized by the government with the help of extreme amounts of aid, including the Christian Youth for Social Services spending hours of time and much money helping dig latrines, bury the dead, and care for the people.

Then pastors had followed up with preaching and teaching in the camps and little groups of believers were being discipled. The movie (which we thought was the dumbest thing we had ever done as missionaries) was now being shown in all the camps to literally thousands of Vietnamese caught in the war. Everyone came, since there was nothing else to do. It was shown in the open air, from the backs of trucks, from a Buddhist temple, and from the steps of makeshift schools.

And God used the movie ... in His timing ... to bring hundreds of Vietnamese to know the strength of His love and to find the Prince of Peace in time of war. Every time we saw it we remembered the funny things we did to "make it happen," but we were thankful to God for His vision and the results that He knew in advance would be realized.

CHAPTER 21

Movie Scenes

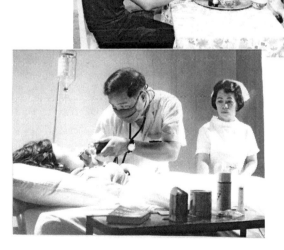

CHAPTER 22

EASTER INVASION 1972

The Paris Peace Accords were ongoing but continually stalled. Chief negotiators for the U.S. (Henry Kissinger) and Vietnam (Le Duc Tho) were determined to stay at the table while both sides continued the conflict. Some American troops had already been withdrawn knowing that the U.S. no longer was willing to continue funding and supply troops. A large base north of Danang city which had held 4,000 troops now sat empty. The Hoa Khanh Children's Hospital was turned over to the World Relief Commission who operated it superbly with U.S. civilian professionals to augment the Vietnamese nursing staff.

As units left, they often came to us with supplies to donate to the mission rather than "deep six" them because they were not permitted to leave things behind or put them into the local economy. One medical unit brought truckloads of medicines which we put into our storeroom for later transport to our mission clinics around the country. We got enough artificial Christmas trees to give to each church in the province and sports equipment for our schools. Many military chaplains had formed relationships with our pastors and church members and found it bittersweet to say good-bye.

In April 1972, the North Vietnamese made a massive ground incursion across the 17th parallel which had divided the north from the south since 1954. They took over the city of Quang Tri and forced the people into the streets. This precipitated an air bombardment that obliterated that province center; not one stone was left on another as the people fled south along Route One. The troops continued toward the old Imperial Capital of Hue pushing thousands of refugees ahead of them across the fabled Hai Van Pass down to our city of Danang. It is estimated that the population of Danang doubled from half a million to one million in less than a week.

During this time, our pastor in Quang Tri, who ran an orphanage, had a "premonition" to send the orphans with his wife to Danang the day before the invasion. They reached Danang in safety. But he and his daughter remained to try to protect the property until he saw it was useless and they raced to make their escape. As they traveled ahead of the tanks and soldiers intent on reaching Hue, they traveled down the highway known as, "The Street Without Joy." It was not the first battle fought there. He later recalled how he and his daughter hid in the ditches along the road, covered with leaves and branches, and described how the feet of the enemy came within inches of them. At one point Pastor Phi dug a "shallow grave" in the dirt and told his daughter it would be their grave or their salvation. Obviously, it was the latter. Later, when Quang Tri province was retaken by government troops, we returned there with Pastor Phi and other missionaries. We could not find any landmark to indicate previous dwellings; it was total rubble. We would later meet many of the Quang Tri people who were among the disenfranchised stragglers who made it to one of the camps in Danang.

The refugees settled where they could. School buildings were overrun. The gates of the school on our property were broken down, and the school which held about 500 students now held over 900 refugees. Some climbed into trucks and stayed there; others fell on the beach if they came by sea. The civilian government worked valiantly; they helped 35,000 refugees settle in the empty American base which had held 4,000 marines. The hospitals were crammed with wounded, disease was rampant due to the contamination of the air and water. There was no adequate sewage disposal or way to bury the many dead. All public functions and services were overwhelmed.

Almost immediately, a well organized group of young adults in the churches banded together and formed an organization called, *"Thanh Nien Co Doc Xa Hoi,"* translated as Christian Youth for Social Services. Since schools and most work places temporarily closed due to the crisis, there were a lot of volunteers. These young men and women began to go to the camps to bury the dead and to dig pit latrines. These two functions are the lowest level of jobs in the Vietnamese culture, so to see these students express their love in this way had a big impact. But even so, the refugees were so desperate without shelter that by night they would come and steal the pieces of tin that had been put around the latrines for privacy.

The leader of these young people, *Thay Do*, saw the desperate need for medical care. He asked me to come to the camp each day with a team to help, especially with the sick children. We could clearly see God's hand in the provision of the wonderful donated medicine which filled our storeroom, which we had not yet transported to our clinics. So each day, two of the other missionary nurses and I would stock our little Mazda station wagon and head for the camp where we would be joined by young Vietnamese men and women who would help us with the set up and manage "crowd control." I not only brought the medications and dressings, but also the table to put them on, a huge water container for drinking, water for wounds, stakes and string to set up a perimeter for treatment, and lots of towels.

Crowd control was impossible. At first we tried to give out numbers, but when we called "Number One," about ten people managed to have their hand on the number. Then we tried eyeing the crowd in a sort of triage that prioritized children. Pushing and shoving was terrible, but we understood it was just the desperation fueling these sick and weary people. The main problem was diarrhea in the children as well as upper respiratory infections, skin infections, and worms. We gave out medication, but obviously did not have enough to give for long-term treatment. We soon realized that hunger, thirst, weariness, and lack of sanitation were the worst problems. And depression, grief and hopelessness were on every face as the past had been obliterated and the future totally obscure.

Big water trucks came to the camp several times daily and the people were able to fill their kettles and containers, but there was never enough to drink freely or for real cleanliness. The temperature hovered over 100 degrees daily and we ourselves mopped our faces constantly as we worked. We brought a thermos of drink for ourselves, but kept it hidden in the vehicle to drink on the way home rather than in front of them. We went to a different site in the camp each day and never "announced" in advance where we would be. We worked until our medicines were gone for the day and then left. It typically lasted about three hours.

One day we saw about four children coming carrying an adult. It turned out that a woman, whose husband was away in the military, badly injured herself while trying to escape with her four children. She stepped on a buried land mine which blew a huge gash in her leg; her children helped her get to the camp. As we unwrapped the rags from her leg, we were appalled. The injury was clear to the bone—jagged and dirty. We packed up our gear, put her in our car with one of her children and went to town to try to get her into the hospital. The overworked doctors there told us there was no chance for her to get anyone's attention unless the leg needed amputation or there was spinal cord involvement; they had no space for a "lesser" problem. The hospital already had two to three patients per bed. They did do an X-Ray at our request to determine that the bones were not compromised, but they could not even clean the wound.

We went back to our car and cleaned and dressed the wound, putting in strong topical medication. We went back to the camp, showed her and her child a "secret place" where we would meet them every second morning, and helped her back to her unit with very little hope. Every second day that we went to the camp we first went to our secret rendezvous. They were always waiting for us. We whisked her into the back seat of the car, stretched out her leg and dressed her wound, never believing that the huge gaping hole would ever heal enough for her to walk. But little by little, it began to close. It was a happy, miraculous day over a month later when we told her the next dressing would be the last. As we approached the spot to meet her, we saw her limping forward with her four children beside her, all scrubbed clean and in their best clothes. They formally gave us thanks for all our loving care and for demonstrating to them the love of Jesus. It was very hard to take the piece of fruit they brought to show their gratitude. And as she limped away, we stood in tears but strangely energized for that day's new challenges.

One day as we finished our treatments (because all the medicines and supplies were gone), we packed up our gear and headed for the car. When I got out my key, it would not go into the keyhole. The opening had been stuffed with little pieces of bamboo and we could not open the doors. The crowd quickly gathered around us and took everything; the empty bottles, the table, the water cooler, and the string and stakes. They melted into the camp and we were left standing by the car. A little boy made a pair of bamboo tweezers and patiently picked out the bamboo. We finally were able to unlock the car, get in, and drive away—angry. "So, that is what they do to us after all we've done for them," was our common thought. Forget it. We won't go back. And we dug out our Kool-Aid and had our long-awaited drinks.

We three nurses were very quiet in the car. Finally, as we neared town, I spoke. I said, "I have never been so needy that I would steal an empty bottle. I cannot condemn these actions toward us without thinking of the great desperation which fueled them. Tomorrow we will go back the same as usual." We did, and we never had that experience again.

One day, the young people told us to come the next day in the afternoon instead of the morning because the president of Vietnam, Nguyen van Thieu, and some officers of the Ministry of Social Services were coming to see what was happening in the camp through our efforts. We were all excited. The next day we wore slightly more attractive dresses, set up a good perimeter, talked to the people, and waited—and waited. All the sick people also waited and we realized it was not right to have all our help available and make them wait, so we began our usual procedures and treated people. One young baby had a terrible cough and as we administered some cough syrup, she gave a horrific heave and coughed the red liquid all down the front of me. As it got hotter, we perspired more and kept working and finally finished with all the medicines and supplies we had brought along—and still no guests.

Just as we were ready to pack up, two helicopters made their appearance and proceeded to land right near us. The dust blew all over and clung to everything, especially the perspiration. What wasn't red was now brown and everything was sticky. As the president and his retinue deplaned and came our way, the leaders called me to talk with him. They introduced me as a nurse who spoke Vietnamese, so he turned to me and asked, "What is wrong with most of these children?" I wanted to say politely that they had diarrhea, but could only think of the colloquial word for it, so blurted it out. Then I tried to cover up my faux pas citing other maladies they had. I got a lot of ribbing because I was on the national equivalent of the "six o'clock news" with my sweaty person and poor Vietnamese language. Later, we got medals and citations from the Ministry of Social Services for our work during those days.

Through all the intense and demanding work, we felt like we made a difference, and that perhaps, just perhaps we were in this country "for such a time as this."

One of the worst tragedies of this period occurred some months after the Easter Invasion at *Que Son* (Cinnamon Mountain) where we had a thriving church under the direction of Pastor and Mrs *Sy* (She). Firebase Ross, an American outpost, stood only two meters from the church, and the chaplains there had cordial relationships with the pastor and congregation. In mid-August 1972, Firebase Ross came under heavy rocket attack. Pastor Sy tells of the events in his own words.

"The next morning Viet Cong appeared near the church. Planes began to bomb them. All the houses in the neighborhood, including those of the Christians, were burned, with the exception of the church and parsonage. The people who were still alive, Christians and non-Christians, ran to the parsonage for refuge—about sixty or seventy people. That evening at about six o'clock two bombs fell next to the parsonage. The church, the parsonage and the youth meeting hall collapsed completely. About thirty people were killed. All the rest were injured, some seriously.

About ten minutes later the Lord led the church treasurer, who had taken shelter about three hundred meters away, to run to the church to remove the beams and bricks from those who were trapped, including my wife, myself and our children. It pleased the Lord that two of our children, My Dung (age 19) and My Duc (14) should return to Him. The church treasurer carried my wife, who was seriously wounded, to the house of a Christian near the district center. I was wounded in the leg and face. Our other children were also wounded.

That night we slept at the home of the Christian where my wife had been taken. The man's family had already left. Bombs were falling in the surrounding area. Nearly all the houses were burned. Although I was wounded, I concerned myself during the night with giving medical help to my wife and other Christians, using the few bandages and medicines which I had carried with me when we fled. On Saturday, August 19 they carried my wife to the district center to try to get her evacuated by helicopter. Because the place was being rocketed no planes could land. Firebase Ross had been abandoned. In the afternoon our national soldiers also abandoned the district center. All day we searched for an escape route but we could find none. Finally Christians carried my wife to the house of a believer who lived near a mountain where we spent the night.

We met Sunday morning, August 20 at 6:00 a.m. to pray. Then my wife and I and several Christians tried again to get out. But the Viet Cong were stopping traffic at many points, so we returned by a round-about way to the mountain. One of my daughters and another Christian girl carried my wife while I hobbled with a cane. We witnessed before our faces the death of many people, but the Lord kept us safe. At one point a Viet Cong drew his gun and shot in the air, but our small children hugged me and said, "Our father is a pastor and he has been wounded. Please don't shoot." The Viet Cong looked at us and let us go. That was the last time we were stopped in the area controlled by the Communists before the Lord led us out to safety." The *Alliance Witness*, November 1972

When they sent this report to us in Danang on September 5, twenty-six Que Son Christians were known dead and twenty others were wounded, some seriously. Seven were captured and fifty-seven were unaccounted for. One hundred and seventeen Christian families lost their homes and all their possessions in the attack. Pastor Sy later died from complications from his wounds. Mrs. Sy recovered and still lives with her daughter in Danang and we had a joyous reunion on one of my recent visits there. In 2010 retired chaplain Marv Eyler, formerly chaplain at Firebase Ross, was planning to visit his friend Pastor Sy in Que Son when he learned the story of the bombing of the church so many years ago. He was able to return and see a congregation of vibrant Christians who meet in a beautiful, newly constructed church. One wall of the new church is from the former church and stands as a memorial to the church family members who perished there.

In April 1972 we witnessed the most emotional, dramatic event in four years already full of heartrending episodes. The Vietnamese government, through the Social Action Committee of the Vietnamese Church, offered three acres of good farmland to any refugee family who was willing to move from the battle-scarred northern area to a planned community four hundred miles south of Danang. Hours of talk and debate took place in countless homes as to whether it was better to risk an immediate new start in a strange place or hope for the possibility of someday being able to return to the homes and fields presently inaccessible.

The Vietnamese are not as mobile as North Americans. They are strongly oriented to their birthplace. Even though the government offered land, transportation, rice for six months and building materials for modest homes, it would be traumatic to leave relatives, regional customs, church friends and ancestral grave sites to go so far away. The proposed settlement area was just seventy-five miles north of Saigon.

About 160 Christian families finally made the momentous decision to go, and they descended on Danang from three neighboring provinces loaded with all their earthly possessions. They arrived on Wednesday, April 11. The Vietnamese Navy boat which was to take them south had been scheduled to leave on Thursday, but there was a five-day delay. Meanwhile, what was to be done with the seven hundred people who were already physically and emotionally exhausted?

The local churches immediately went into action. They housed the people in a school building next to one of the churches, and organized them into groups with appointed leaders. One pastor became responsible for feeding the people. Even though some of them had a little food, everything they had was packed into the already stowed crates to go to the new destination. Most of them had nothing at all.

Another pastor cared for a medical aid station and another for administration. Still another provided spiritual ministries, including a daily morning prayer service and evening vespers. As soon as we assessed the desperate situation our hearts went out to these precious men, women and children of the household of faith. We phoned our Saigon headquarters for permission to use emergency funds. With these funds we provided a daily rice ration for each person, a cow which was butchered for fresh meat for a farewell dinner before they boarded the ship and a two-pound tin of canned meat for each family for the three-day trip. Other organizations provided bread, medicine, soap, and a blanket per family, and a pig for the farewell dinner. The Danang city government gave each person the equivalent of about $1.00 U.S. to show their concern and interest in this group exodus. Our own household made Vietnamese doughnuts and provided bananas to supplement the diet.

A farewell service was held Monday evening following the feast. Christians from all over the city gathered to share in this with their brethren. It was characterized by a sense of unity and love. The keynote message promised that amid all the uncertainty and sense of loss, they could be assured that God was with them. We could almost see the negative feelings change to expectancy, excitement and hope. A Communion service climaxed the farewell meeting.

And then—more delay! The LST-type naval boat was rescheduled for Tuesday—and then Wednesday. Orders came for the refugees to embark Wednesday at 8:00 a.m., and mass confusion resulted as Army trucks loaded people, dogs, possessions, and well-wishers and took them to the dock area. In the midst of this the mayor and civic leaders had a dockside farewell meeting. By mid-afternoon things sorted themselves out. We found about a third of the families under a makeshift shelter on the open deck and the others, fearing the elements, in the incredibly hot hold along with the baggage and equipment. Every nook and cranny held a family unit, including the gun turrets, stair ramps and beneath the lifeboats. One pastor, perhaps feeling a bit like Moses, went along to shepherd the people, and one wealthy layman was so moved by the sight of his brave fellow-Christians that he volunteered to go to share in the trip with them. How moving to read the huge banner placed on the bridge of the ship, "Let us love one another as God for Christ's sake loves us."

Then tragedy struck! Minutes before the boat left, two seventeen-year-old boy cousins were leaning on a wire-rope railing when the rope snapped, dropping them right before our eyes into the water between the boat and the pier. The Vietnamese navy seamen were in the water immediately with life preservers. One boy bobbed up and was saved. The other boy did not surface. He had hit his head on the wharf in falling and went into the water unconscious and drowned. His body was recovered by a diver shortly after the boat left the pier at 6:30 p.m. So the boat left in the midst of tragedy. Tears were in every eye.

Our Christian brethren were leaving their homes and all they knew, to go to an area about which they knew nothing. But they were committed and they knew the One who was with them. So after days and years of hardship, seven days in Danang, and thirty-six hours on the ship, they would arrive in a better land. Their new village was named *Phuc Am Binh Tuy*, Gospel Village.

I recently learned that about ten years ago an American organization called International Cooperating Ministries helped this congregation rebuild their 1,000 seat church right on Highway One. Today, the membership of Gospel Village Church is over 3,000. Truly God did lead them to a Promised Land.

CHAPTER 22

Quảng Trị Rubble
"The Street Without Joy"

Refugees streaming into Danang clog the city's thoroughfares

The
Big
Move

November 22, 1972

Children of Rev. and Mrs. Nguyen-van-Sy at memorial service for their two sisters, whose bodies remain buried in rubble that once was Que Son Evangelical Church. My Dung's picture is on the table.

Christian refugees in the Danang area of Viet Nam utilize former U.S. Marine chapel for training class in witness and church leadership. Tribes pastors, themselves refugees from the fighting in the northern provinces, are finding many of the refugees ripe for evangelism. W. C. Stemple

This son of Pastor and Mrs. Sy was missing for five days before he turned up safe, having been passed from one person to another

Quế Sơn Church

CHAPTER 23

WOODY AND HIS WHEELCHAIRS

Over the years of fighting, the wounded and disabled Vietnamese veterans had become a very visible and fearsome "sub-population." Their numbers continually increased, but their pensions were woefully inadequate. In addition, they lacked proper care and could not find meaningful work. They banded together in united fashion in the larger cities and sometimes organized with leaders and terrorized the civilian population. For example, in Danang they would go to restaurants or movie theaters and insist on a free meal or a free ticket. If denied, they would pull the pin on a grenade and threaten the management, which action usually got them their request.

These *thuong phe binh* (wounded veterans) would sometimes take advantage of the "squatters' rights law" which said in essence that if a piece of vacant property had a house with a roof on it, the property under the roof belonged to the owner of the house. Of course, this law was meant for the protection of long-term inhabitants of unknown or disputed land. But these wounded veterans had a great scheme: a group of them would come in during the night and put four poles with a thatch roof on to a homeowners' front yard or property and then declare it as their own, according to squatters rights. The owner would then have the choice of buying his land back or co-existing with the shack. They took over lovely beachfronts on this clever premise, as they did the land along our front wall. Inside our four foot high decorative wall was peace and quiet; on the other side the market loomed above and beyond our wall with its noise and color.

Groups of the disabled men would sometimes ride side by side down the streets in wheelchairs slashing tires on cars or staging demonstrations for more rights to their care. Their families were usually their only caregivers, as the need overwhelmed the government. Naturally, not every wounded veteran followed this destructive path, but enough of them did to make them another strong bloc in the mosaic of groups in Vietnam during those hectic days.

From the beginning of our ministry in Quang Ngai we had worked with the wounded Vietnamese soldiers, often visiting in the military hospital across the street. Our colleagues in Saigon and Nhatrang and other cities had also established regular visiting and teaching ministries in their military hospitals. Many non-government organizations (NGOs) also helped. For instance, World Vision was providing wheelchairs; Bible Literature International was providing magazines, New Testaments and other reading materials; and individual churches sent toiletries and gift packages for the wounded.

So, when we returned to Danang, we naturally explored this avenue of ministry. The large veteran's hospital in Danang welcomed us warmly, as they had overwhelming need. Woody became the distributor of wheelchairs for World Vision and that one aspect of his life almost took over everything else. The requirements for getting a chair would be that the veteran was totally paralyzed from his waist down, or be a bilateral amputee with at least one of the legs amputated above the knee. One missing leg was not "enough." This meant that each person requesting a wheelchair would have to submit an application with a photo and Woody would then submit that name for the next distribution, if he met all the requirements.

Each distribution would include a big ceremony at the hospital meeting room filled with folding chairs for the participants. About one hundred shiny new wheelchairs would be lined up across the front and participants would be wheeled in on beds or hospital chairs or propped on the folding chairs with a caregiver. Large armchairs would make up the front row where the visiting dignitaries would sit. This would include the head Vietnamese general of I Corps, the head of the hospital and some top staff, Woody and me, if present. At the end of the impressive ceremony, the names would be called and the wheelchairs distributed. We felt fulfilled and validated when we saw the joy in the recipient's face. The wheelchair meant everything for his future.

The more we gave, the more the wounded poured in. The general actually seconded a room in the hospital for an office for Woody. To staff the office the General appointed a young Christian military recruit, who had once been a student pastor, to do the paperwork and oversee the office. This Vietnamese soldier was unique: paid by the military, approved by the Tin Lanh church district, and working under the direction of a U.S. civilian—Woody. His presence greatly relieved our work load. Woody only retained control of the final approval of each chair. Eventually a small chapel was built on the military hospital grounds for services.

Because the chairs were made for sidewalks and hospital corridors, and because the men rode them in the streets, country lanes and rice fields, they only lasted a few years. So we began to get requests for new chairs from men who already had one. We simply did not have enough chairs to give seconds, but the men creatively submitted false names with their photos. Woody really loved the men and had a knack for remembering them well, so very few got past him for a second chair—as far as we know, that is.

The need was overwhelming and people flooded Woody with requests. One time after a distribution at the hospital we were going out of the ward when we found veterans lying on the sidewalk where we intended to walk. They were protesting because they had been waiting so long for chairs and did not receive one that day. They said they would lie there until they got a chair and we would have to step on them to leave the area. Our hearts broke for them but we could not do more. The general became very upset at this lack of control and we feared the situation would get worse. A way was cleared for us to pass and such an incident did not happen again.

The chairs were not ideal for conditions in Vietnam and several organizations were working on better, adaptable, sustainable chairs which could be made of local materials, such as bicycle tires instead of the metal rims. But the physics of self propelling remained unsolved, and also no one had produced near the volume needed. So Woody decided he would open a "wheelchair repair shop" in our backyard. I had a fit. For one thing, did he know how to repair wheelchairs? Well, he could fix a car and he figured a chair would be a lot easier. Could he do this by himself? A young airplane mechanic from the Air Force base heard about the idea and promised to come each week on Wednesday, his day off, and help Woody. Where would he get the parts? The wheelchair company offered to sell them to him at 30% off with free shipping. The chaplains offered him the use of their military postal system to receive the parts. Who would pay for them? He had no answer for that, but knew it was God's plan for him. The U.S. chaplains began to take offerings in their chapel programs to help pay for the parts. One by one, my arguments were answered. But my biggest fear was that we would be overrun by these veterans; that they would show up every day. They might cause havoc and destruction in our yard, or even become squatters on our tiny square of grass where the repairs would take place.

Really, as soon as Woody got the idea, things fell into place. Before I knew it, he announced through his military contacts, his on-base office, and the "bamboo grapevine" that he would begin on Wednesdays at eight o'clock behind our house. That next week I waited in apprehension as he set up his "shop," set out his first shipment of parts, and arranged for Mike Nylin to come in from the base. And the veterans came. They came early, but never came any day but Wednesday. Most of them were carried in by friends since their wheelchairs were unusable. They came carrying pieces, parts and battered wheels, but they were all respectful.

Most of the chairs had ruined bearings (due to running on so much sand), torn canvas seats or backs, and bent or broken wheels. As Woody and Mike worked, the men talked among themselves, amazed that Americans of the "teacher class" were doing this mechanical work. I took them lemonade to drink, and they sat and read the material about the real reason we were in Vietnam that we had piled in the "waiting area." And they got it. As the year went on, Woody's great satisfaction was hearing the new ones ask the ones who had come before, "Why does he do this?" And the ones who knew would answer that God's love was the motivation. They "gossiped the gospel" in our backyard and Woody did not have to "preach" at all.

Our kids loved Wednesdays. They got to try out the newly repaired chairs with the guys. The owner would sit on the chair and the kids would either push it or crawl up on their lap for a test ride. They never seemed to notice that the vet had no legs, or no feeling; they just saw the happy smiles and welcome camaraderie in our backyard.

And me? I became a believer! Every time a bill came for parts, a chaplain from some unit would show up at the door. He would ask Woody if he had any project that needed funds, or he had already heard about the outdoor repair shop, or for some other unexplainable reason he had ready cash—and we never missed a payment. My real shame came the Wednesday a motorized wheelchair came zooming into our driveway. A fearsome long-haired, bearded, man with a scar all across his face called to me. As I approached him, he introduced himself as the head of the I Corps disabled veterans and said, "I just wanted you to know we had a division meeting last night and we have placed your family under our protection. No harm will come to you, your family or your property because of all you have done for the veterans." Okay, Lord, I get it.

In the midst of all this, we were overwhelmed by requests for help for the total paraplegics. There was little adequate care and no long-term solution for these wounded men who could not move at all. Through a large gift from the Kathryn Kuhlman Foundation, Woody offered to oversee the construction of a twelve-bed paraplegic ward in the military hospital. It had twelve Stryker frame beds, all the necessary equipment, air conditioning and TVs. It was well received and a wonderful help for the care and post-trauma recovery of Vietnamese soldiers.

Woody was inducted as an honorary citizen of the City of Danang by the mayor. He received a medal for his wheelchair ministry given by the head Vietnamese general of I Corps. But nothing made us happier than to be in town and see rows of our wheelchairs racing down the streets and smiling friends waving at us everywhere we went. Great thanks goes to the organizations who made it possible, to Mike with his weekly help, to the wheelchair company and their discounted parts, to countless GIs who paid the bills, to our mission for authenticating this ministry, to Woody's vision, and to God who thought it all up in the first place.

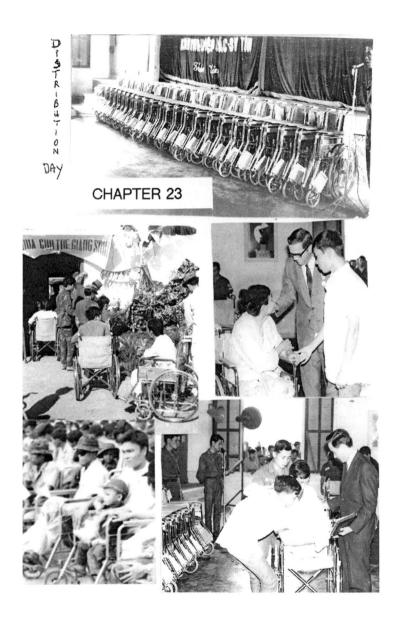

CHAPTER 23

General and
Mrs. Lâm

Mike Nylin

Repair Shop

(decree of citizenship
by mayor of Danang)

Woody honored

CHAPTER 24

THE LAST YEAR

One sunny day our hospitality became severely strained. Even though our four-year term was winding down, we ourselves were still racing at full-tilt. For the previous calendar year we had recorded over 2000 guest meals served and had well over 200 overnight guests. Because so many groups helped with projects and funding, they sent representatives to document their work and we flourished as the "best hotel" in town. Thankfully, our household workers also enjoyed having these visitors.

But that day, I opened the front door (which no one ever used) to find a navy officer who introduced himself as the chaplain from a naval carrier ship, The New Orleans. My eyes widened as behind him I could see military uniforms clear out to the street. He must have sensed my confusion as his next words were, "Didn't you get my message?" Apparently his ship was out in Danang Harbor, he had heard about us and he had asked how many men wanted to go with him to work at the local mission in Danang. Over forty sailors volunteered, so he then sent us that message via some land-based chaplain. Since our local telephone seldom worked, we depended on word of mouth for messages and, no, we hadn't gotten his.

After a big gulp, we had them all come in, called our wonderful yardman Mr. Le, and asked about "duty" for these guys. We managed to round up enough paint and repair jobs to keep them busy for the day. Most of them were more interested in going out the driveway to the market to buy souvenirs. They had brought their own dark green cans of C-rations to eat, but they were happy to leave them with us as our wonderful Chi Hai made an authentic Vietnamese meal for them all. In the end, we referred to that day as "the invasion."

The hardest day of that year for us was the happiest day for Stewart. It was the day he got to go away to school. When he was five years old, he had attended the local Vietnamese Baptist kindergarten and had a great year. Each fall, he had watched the other missionary kids take off for "real school" by airplane and he longed to join them. Due to the fact that there was no adequate English-language schooling for missionary children, the Alliance had established a boarding school in 1929 in Dalat, Vietnam. In 1965 the U.S. Embassy had decided that they could no longer risk having over 200 American students in one vulnerable location, so the school had been evacuated. With the help of the U.S. military, all students, faculty and equipment flew to a new location in Bangkok Thailand over that Easter weekend.

After one semester in Bangkok, the school relocated to the cooler Cameron Highlands in Malaysia and "took over" a small hotel there. It was ideal in climate and surroundings, but too far removed from good medical care or large-scale purchases. A former British R&R center on Penang Island off the west coast of Malaysia became available, so the Dalat school rented "Sandycroft" from the current owners and moved once again. During the 1990s the mission policy changed completely and has turned all of its missionary children schools over to private ownership and boards. Today, Dalat School continues to flourish in Penang as a fully accredited American school with an enrollment of over 400, which serves both the local and international community.

So, in the fall of 1972 Stewart was ready to go to Penang. It was all he talked about for months, as we prepared his clothing with name tags and tried to prepare ourselves for the separation. As he flew from Danang to Saigon and then raced to the plane with about 40 other Vietnam missionary children, he was living his dream to be with all the other kids he knew at the fabled Dalat. But it was hard. Those were different days from now and we did not have home schooling options or curricula; we had known from the beginning this would happen; but it was still hard. We knew the wonderful and dedicated dorm parents who cared for him, so that made it a bit easier. He wrote the obligatory letter home (with help) each Sunday, and he enjoyed himself there immensely from all reports.

Within six weeks we went to see him. As missionaries we received a month's vacation annually but because there were so few safe places to "vacation" in Vietnam, the mission helped us go out of the country every 18 months. Earlier we had taken this stipend and gone to Hong Kong and Taiwan to visit friends. Now that we had a child at Penang, there was no question where we would go. But we chose a fun way to get there. We booked passage for three on a freighter stopping in Saigon. Since they already had nine passengers, we took the final three places, as freighters could only carry a maximum of twelve passengers.

We boarded in Saigon and paid for a five day trip to Singapore; from there we planned to take a train to Penang. However, the freighter stopped in Thailand and took on freight for Indonesia, so we crossed the equator and unexpectedly visited Jakarta, and then back; it took us eight days (for the price of five). The other passengers had heard that "missionaries" were getting on the ship and were quite concerned we would somehow ruin their fun. In the end, I took the passengers sightseeing in Bangkok and Jakarta to places they would never have seen. Woody stayed on the ship with Sam, thankful to have a quiet place to rest and enjoy. Three-year-old Sam became the recipient of everyone's love, attention and gifts—and I … I had an automatic washer and dryer right next to our cabin and I pushed those buttons like a happy mama every single day.

The halcyon ship days ended and we took the overnight train from Singapore to Penang. From the train station to the school we went by cab with our anticipation building beyond belief. Stewart knew when we would come, so it was not a surprise. We arrived at the school, found his dorm, learned he was out playing and rushed to the area. There he was and we called his name, "HI, STEWART." He turned around, saw us, waved, and kept playing. Ouch!

He took us for a tour of the school and introduced us to his second grade teacher, Mrs. Livingston. This was our first big surprise—we learned he had tested so well that the staff and counselors had recommended he skip first grade, which turned out to be a great decision both academically and socially. When we mentioned that we wished they had contacted us about this decision, they pointed out the reality that we were coming to visit before we could get mail back and forth. We took Stewart to a hotel for the weekend where we had him all to ourselves and had a great visit. We came back to Danang well-rested and confident of an excellent school situation for our son, even though we still missed him terribly.

Coincidentally, our lives would take a turn so that we would actually be serving at Dalat School after Vietnam fell to the Communists. Stewart would be back at Dalat living on the campus as a "staff student" from grades 4-9. When we moved to the U.S. he spent grades 10-11 with us, and then came back to Dalat for his senior year as a "private student" to graduate as "Student of the Year" in 1983. This was his desire and his choice, so we were glad we could make it possible, even though it was still hard! Sam also later attended Dalat School in Penang, but as a "staff student," not a boarding student.

Our last Christmas in Vietnam we had a young marine come as an unexpected visitor. He came to our house a few days before Christmas to bring some used clothing his mother had sent to us. She had been sending clothing for over five years and now that her son was in the area, she asked him to bring it to us. He *very obviously* did not relish the idea of visiting "the missionaries" and had put it off until almost the end of his deployment. He stood uncomfortably in our doorway in his fatigues looking around as if to see if anyone was watching. He had gotten permission to go off base on R&R and stopped off at our place on the way to the beach. We invited him in, raved about his Mom's faithful donations, and gave him some home-baked goodies. He saw our Christmas decorations, realized we had an island of normality in the middle of the busy city, and began to relax. He actually got down on the floor and played with our kids; he now seemed in no hurry to go.

We invited him to stay for supper and a Christmas program at the church next door that evening. He had no other clothes to wear, but after Woody offered to loan him some civvies, he agreed. He not only stayed for the program, he then agreed to stay overnight. We located his chaplain and explained where he was and that he might actually stay the whole three days with us, which the chaplain agreed to endorse.

That night, we sat talking late. Woody went on to bed and the young man continued talking to me. Suddenly, it was as though he did not even realize I was there; he poured out his heart about the things he had seen and done as "point man" in his unit. He began to talk to others in his unit; to call out about what should have been and could have been;

to get his uniform and empty his pockets of his "war souvenirs," and then he began to cry. I was witnessing a miraculous catharsis. He had become a boy again and not a soldier, and when he finished sobbing he looked at me and suddenly realized where he was. The peace of God, Christmas and our home seemed to settle on him and he said, "I think I'll go to bed now." We had a wonderful three days together and he was a great Christmas gift to us all.

That same Christmas the youth choir lined up outside the church waiting for their time to sing, when a stray bullet shot into the air by a nearby Christmas celebrant came down and grazed the skull of one of the young women in line. She fell to the ground with blood spurting profusely from her head causing the choir to go into disarray and grief. A fast examination showed it had only grazed her skull, so she was bandaged up and even able to stand and sing. It reminded us that our world may have been miles from "Peace on Earth, Goodwill to Men," but we celebrated that Christmas with a "Joy to the World" ending.

One more event marked that memorable Christmas. After a non-stop day of Christmas programs and events, each a "production" in its own right, we had come home exhausted. About ten o'clock the pastor from our "end-of-the-runway" church came knocking on our door. He said that a family in the "sandspit refugee camp" wanted us to come to a big dinner that they had prepared. We were incredulous that we were expected to go out again, but the pastor insisted that one of us go, so I agreed. Two pastors, one pastor's wife and I went to the edge of the river where we crossed a footbridge out to a "sandspit" or small islet in the middle of the river.

We were familiar with the refugees who had landed on this place after the Easter invasion. It was a small area and devoid of building material so they all had built their houses out of discarded American cardboard. We actually called it the "cardboard camp." Their places looked like they were playing house with the carton their fridge or washer came in, but it was their only shelter. A pastor had visited these people, given them a message of hope, and a small group of believers had formed. They had a tiny plywood church there where they worshipped and a family of believers had invited us to come.

We stooped over and entered the cardboard home lit by kerosene lamps. By now it was almost midnight, but they were prepared for us. There was a makeshift table made from ammunition packing crates with little three-legged stools placed beside it for the four guests and the host. As I sat on my stool it sank right into the sand. I felt like I was on a picnic. Then the sweet wife of the home began bringing in wonderful dishes to us; and lots of them—all cooked over a small charcoal fire. They combined donated rice and wheat with miscellaneous C-rations and fresh market food. A meal appeared that I could not have managed with my double oven and microwave! As we shared the delicious meal together, our host told us this remarkable story.

He was in the Vietnamese navy and his patrol boat was out at sea when the invasion occurred. He learned by radio that Quang Tri, his home province, had been overrun by the North Vietnamese and then bombed to smithereens. As soon as he could get to shore he began searching for his wife and two children. He could find no landmarks in Quang Tri, so he followed the refugee trail down through Hue to Danang and finally found out that his neighborhood people had ended in the sandspit camp, if they had survived. He was afraid to find out their status, and if he did find them alive, he was sure they would be despondent and ill because of their total loss and lack of help.

When he found his wife, he was shocked. She was happy, healthy, and eager to tell him of her journey. Yes, they had lost everything, but she assured him they had found something far more valuable—a relationship with the God of the universe. Skeptical, he visited the local pastor and heard the good news of the gospel, which he also received. Together, they spent his leave time learning and growing in their new-found faith. Just before he had to go back to sea, he told her, "We need to give God a gift as thanks for what He has done for us." Without anyone asking him, without any teaching on "tithing," and without any idea how they would survive, they gratefully gave God a large gift from his wages through their local church and pastor.

Shortly after he returned to sea, at least fourteen miles offshore they felt something big bump their patrol boat in the middle of the night. Startled, the sailors on board tried to see what it was, then there was another bump. There were never any fish of that large size so they were perplexed as it happened yet again. They got their gaff hooks and tried to figure out what was happening; everywhere they poked, there were huge objects. Finally pulling one in close, they discovered it was a 100-kilo sack of rice. They hauled one into the boat, then the next, and the next until they nearly swamped the boat. They took the sacks in to shore and turned them in to the government, another miracle. The government gave them a big reward with their explanation.

At this time the United States had an embargo on ships coming into North Vietnam. So the Russians were floating large waterproof bags of rice past the embargo into the port. But God caused a storm to float these bags of rice hundreds of miles south to bump into the small boat of a tithing man right in the middle of the ocean. This dinner was a celebration to thank God for the huge reward the man had gotten. I will not forget his wise words, "I have learned that you cannot outgive God." What a Christmas lesson.

Right up to the time we left Vietnam we busied ourselves with refugee ministries and working with the district superintendent and pastors. With God's help we completed a lovely district headquarters building next to the superintendent's home. It included downstairs offices, a large bookstore/reading room, and upstairs rooms where visitors could stay overnight when they came in from the country.

The large numbers of American military had all left after the Paris Peace Accords were signed in 1973 but the Vietnamese government troops continued the fight against the ever present Viet Cong. At the end of the Dalat school term, Stewart came home from school and we packed up for our 12-month home assignment. We left all our furniture, household items, books, and lessons in storage for our anticipated return in one year. Our beloved Vietnamese church leaders and friends gave us a wonderful farewell and we flew home to our waiting families.

CHAPTER 24

Stewart's
Second Grade

Sam on the
"cruise"

Phu Loc Chapel

Dedication of Bridge - Phu Loc Camp - "Sandspit"

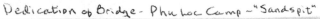

CHAPTER 25

TRANSITION

A huge, unexpected, unwanted change awaited us at the end of our year of home assignment. We had a wonderful year at "Beulah Beach" on Lake Erie west of Cleveland. We were in much demand as speakers since we had the "inside" story on Viet Nam. We visited lots with grandmas and grandpas, and Stewart had third grade in Vermilion, Ohio. But our hearts longed for Danang; so near the end of summer 1974, we packed our things in 55-gallon drums, produced a newsletter with our information and included a five-year wallet calendar with our picture on it so people would pray for us. We purchased our tickets, and made our plans to return.

A few weeks before we were to leave, our national mission headquarters called us to ask us if we would please take a two-year break from Viet Nam and go instead to Dalat School in Penang Malaysia to be house parents. It seems there had been "issues" at the school, and "people" felt we would do a good job. Woody said, "NO, thank you." He added that he was "called to preach and not care for other people's children." Case closed. But, meanwhile, I had to have minor surgery which delayed our return, and in that time, they called again. Now, they offered the job of chaplain <u>and</u> house parents, so Woody could preach. They felt that this was the right thing; they promised we could go to Danang and say our good-byes en route to Penang and then come back every vacation to Vietnam. It was ONLY FOR TWO YEARS. So, we agreed.

We went kicking and screaming internally to Dalat School on Penang Island, just off the west coast of Malaysia. A multi-cultural, modern, cosmopolitan environment with world-class beaches, excellent transportation and wonderful food soon won our hearts. The setting on the Indian Ocean was spectacular; we could be with both our children, and the school warmly welcomed us. We settled into the incredibly busy life of dorm parenting and the chaplaincy. Our apartment was right in the middle of our dorm; full of twenty-eight boys from grade one to twelve. The senior high boys scared me at first, but before long, I scared them! Actually, it became a mutual love affair that ended up lasting six years, but that is another story.

At Christmas, we were permitted to return to Vietnam. The celebration of the holiday plus several other special meetings where we ministered gave us great satisfaction. But we could sense more tension. We heard it was no longer safe for a missionary to live in our beloved Quang Ngai, for example. As we accompanied the thirty-five Vietnam missionary children back to Penang after the holidays, we actually felt a bit relieved to leave safely.

By February 1975 reports were coming in of the communist infiltration of outlying villages and provinces. The Viet Cong were bolder and government centers were unable to hold them off. Slowly but surely, the North Vietnamese forces began to take over and our missionaries in outlying cities and towns moved into larger centers. In March we heard on the radio of the fall of our beloved Quang Ngai which devastated us. Many Vietnamese, who had ties with the Americans through work or social relationships felt compromised and had to flee their homes.

It is impossible to chronicle the slow but steady change in status, but by April 1, most of our missionaries had packed up their suitcases and moved to Nhatrang and then down to Saigon. Each one had his own story. This included the missionaries in our new language school in Dalat. Each one hoped they would get back when the "current situation" improved.

This was a monumental time for us at Dalat School. As the missionaries had been leaving their homes, decisions were being made with our mission in concert with the U.S. embassy. If the evacuees were single or a family with no school-age children, they were sent home to the United States or Canada. If they had children at Dalat School, they were sent to Penang. The mission gave them housing in a small hotel near the school for the two months until the end of the semester to keep a semblance of normalcy. We were able to love and comfort our colleagues, to share meals with them, and to pray together for those beloved ones left behind. We began to understand a bit about why God had "sent us ahead" to Penang.

On March 12, during a week-long battle for the strategic mountain town of Banmethuot, the North Vietnamese captured seven missionaries and took them away. This included Alliance personnel Dick and Lillian Phillips, Norm and Joan Johnson, and Betty Mitchell, as well as Wycliffe translators John and Carolyn Miller with their five-year-old daughter LuAnne. As this shocking news hit the school, we knew for sure why we were there. Dick and Lil had four children at the school, one of whom was in our Grade One dorm room right next to our apartment. The two Johnson teen-agers knew us well from our mutual home in Danang and Gerry Mitchell, a junior in high school, knew we understood her situation and her love for Vietnam. The entire student body, as well as the staff and workers, prayed for these parents-in-captivity and for colleagues still serving in the country as daily decisions affected all our lives.

On the fateful morning of April 30, 1975, the North Vietnamese tanks drove into Saigon and through the gates of the presidential palace. The three-day President of South Vietnam surrendered, and the rest is history. In those final days our last missionaries escaped, some on the very last helicopter to leave from the roof of the American Embassy. The "Vietnam Era" was over for the military as well as for the missionaries.

It had been the custom of Lil Phillips, one of the captives, to send a package for each of her four children to open every Sunday during the 18 weeks of the semester. She sent all these ahead to the house parents at the beginning of the term, so it was bittersweet to give John and Bryan, her sons, their Sunday packages. John lost about five teeth those few months, so I kept them wrapped in a little box as a sort of guarantee that I could send them to his mother one day soon. Meanwhile, there was no word at all about the whereabouts or condition of the captives. All diplomatic efforts came to nothing. Gerry Mitchell, whose mother was taken, had also lost her father to Vietnamese captors in 1962 when he was taken with two other Americans from the leprosarium in Banmethuot. They had not been heard from since and were presumed dead.

As the semester ended and the weary, waiting families took their children to go home to find new ministry, decisions had to be made about the seven children at the school whose captive parents were still missing with no news of them at all. They wanted to remain at familiar Dalat and the staff was more than willing to care for them over the summer, but the decision was made to send six of them home to the families that had been designated in the wills to care for them. Every missionary who serves overseas with the

Christian and Missionary Alliance has to have a will, and it would have to include the "disposition" of the children in the case of the loss of both parents. So the four Phillips children and two Johnson children went home to family caregivers. Gerry was permitted to stay at Dalat since she had only one year until graduation. We were so glad.

In October 1975 the Vietnamese released the missionary prisoners from the infamous "Hanoi Hilton" in a prisoner exchange, and they came home via Bangkok to great fanfare and joy. I sent Johnnie's teeth to Lil Phillips and told her of God's pledge to me that she would get them and that she owed the "tooth fairy" five dollars! Betty Mitchell came to Dalat and served as dietitian while Gerry completed High School and then stayed on to minister there.

Meanwhile, after the communist takeover—called "the revolution" by the victors—no Americans were allowed in Vietnam, and to this day, no missionary or "religious worker" visas have been granted. And for the Vietnamese people remaining, traditional freedoms were few. It has been estimated that 65,000 Vietnamese were executed after the end of the war with one million being sent to prison/re-education camps where an estimated 165,000 died. Many took the drastic decision to leave the country—an illegal act under the communist government. This became a whole new chapter in our relationship with our beloved Vietnamese people. [1]

---

[1] For statistics of post-Vietnam war deaths and imprisonment see Chapter 11 "The Vietnamese War State" in: Rummel, Rudolf J. *Death by Government*. New Brunswick: Transition Publishers, 1994. Print.

CHAPTER 25

home in Ohio
1974

The Norm Johnson Family

CHAPTER 26

"...AND SHE WRAPPED HIM IN SWADDLING CLOTHES AND LAID HIM IN A MANGER, BECAUSE THERE WAS NO ROOM FOR THEM IN THE INN."

CHAPTER 26

THE BOAT PEOPLE

Immediately after the fall of Vietnam, the victorious communists rounded up all those who were in the military, especially the officers, plus any civilians who had close ties to American or other western agencies. As conditions deteriorated in post-war Vietnam and air flight out of the country became impossible, many took to makeshift boats in an effort to flee and start a new life elsewhere. Fishing boats crammed with people and totally unsuitable for the open seas set off over rough waters seeking asylum.

No one really knows how many people made the decision to flee by boat, however, the number who attempted this has been put as high as 1.5 million. Estimates for deaths vary from 50,000 to 200,000 (Australian Immigration Ministry). The primary cause of death was drowning, although many refugees suffered brutal attacks by pirates with many murdered, or sold into slavery and prostitution. Some countries in the region, such as Malaysia, turned the boat people away even if they did manage to land. Boats carrying the refugees were deliberately sunk offshore by those in them to stop the authorities towing them back to sea. But, because the east coast of Malaysia was a natural landing place for the boats and the first one arrived in May 1975, something had to be done. [1]

In 1978 the Malaysian government and UNHCR (U.N. High Commission for Refugees) set up a refugee camp for Vietnamese "Boat People" on Bidong Island. Pulau Bidong was a small, uninhabited island situated off the coast of Terengganu State in the South China Sea where boats which floated into Malaysian waters would be sent or towed. There the refugees would fill out paperwork and await interviews with representatives of the "third countries" which they hoped would find a place for them. Vietnam was the "first country" or country of origin; Malaysia was the "second country" or host country; and the destination was called the third country. Totaling all Vietnamese refugees, the United States accepted 823,000 refugees; Britain accepted 19,000; France accepted 96,000; Australia and Canada accepted 137,000 each. [1]

When refugees were processed on Bidong and fully accepted into a third country, they were sent to a transit camp called "Sungei Besi," located in the capital city of Malaysia—Kuala Lumpur. There they had medical tests, immunizations, X-Rays, and were briefed on what to expect in their future home. They also received the location where they would be going and airplane tickets for themselves and their families. This was the only site within Malaysia where refugees were permitted and it was well guarded and controlled. Ideally, they would only be there two weeks, but it sometimes took longer to complete the paperwork.

Woody and I had visited Sungei Besi twice. We had gotten official permission to go and see some Christians we had known in Vietnam when we learned from their relatives that they were there. Although the conditions in the transit center were crowded and unsanitary, they were a step up on the road to freedom. Our refugee friends there were full of hope at the prospect of a new life, which they hoped would wipe out the terrible memories of the escape which included surviving a raid by Thai pirates in the Gulf of Thailand. Their stories were simply one of hundreds, but at least now they were "accepted" by another country and could look ahead.

Although we were at Dalat School, off the west coast of the Malay Peninsula, our daily papers were full of the plight of the Vietnamese refugees off the east coast. Betty Mitchell and I developed a desire to go to the camp and see the situation, but trying to get access to Bidong Island remained very difficult. We heard rumors that 25,000 Vietnamese currently lived on the island. One day a friend visiting Penang who was in charge of all the voluntary agencies working with the refugee project told us, "It's easy now to get permission to go to Bidong," and he gave us the name of a man to ask. We wanted to go during the Christmas holidays to encourage the Christian believers.

We soon found out it was NOT easy to get there; many people had to give their permissions. Finally, after turning in lots of paperwork, making a flurry of phone conversations between us and the immigration department, and with a friend working frantically all Christmas Eve Day to expedite everything, we got permission to go for two days. We planned to go on a Friday, but early in the week realized that Terengganu State was predominantly Muslim, which would mean that Friday would be their Holy Day and perhaps the offices would be closed. It was a busy holiday travel time and we could not get a Thursday flight, but, at the last minute we were able to change our plane tickets to go Thursday to Kota Baru State, where we took a taxi three hours south to Terengannu. Little did we realize this would be just one of the "miraculous" things that would end up making our trip a reality.

On a Thursday morning we flew in a small plane across the Malaysian Peninsula to the city of Kota Baru where we bought the back seat of a taxi (for about $10.00 US) and rode the three hours south to Terengganu. We had been given the name of a hotel to stay in and told to go see the "Task Force Officer" for instructions. A U.N. boat went to the island each morning and came back each evening, we were told. Originally, I had the naïve idea that we would just go to the dock and rent a boat to take us there—things were far more tightly controlled than I had imagined.

From this point on, our trip took on elements of a spy thriller. After checking into our hotel about 2:00 p.m. we found out that in Terengganu Thursday is a half-day preceding the Friday off—their weekend—and nothing was likely to be open. We took our paperwork and went to find the Task Force office. This huge building was totally deserted; the lone security guard told us they were closed until Saturday. We asked about the U.N. office and he told us how to find it way across town. We took trishaws there. The trishaw seemed strange to us since the bike peddler rides beside you; in Vietnam they ride behind you; in other countries they ride in front of you. At any rate, we prayed all the way that the UN offices would be open, and they were.

Although surprised to see two Americans on their doorstep, everyone at the U.N. office wanted to help us. They sent us to "Ali" who looked at our papers. These said we had a permit to go to Bidong on Saturday and Sunday, but he said, "Sorry, there are no boats going those days. If you want to go Friday, you can." YES! We had come a day early and thus would get the only boat for the weekend. We agreed. First he had to call CID (Civil Investigative Division—the police) for their permission. Ali informed us the police would come to our hotel at 10:30 p.m. to check our paperwork. If there were no problems we should be at the unfinished wharf a few miles outside the city at 8:00 a.m. the next day, and wait for a boat called "Black Gold."

Betty and I walked down to the beach for supper at a nice hotel on the water rejoicing that we were still getting green lights. We went shopping in a sundry store and bought ten bags of peanuts and cookies and a five-pound packet of tea. We had already been told we could not distribute anything on the island without permission, but at least we could bring some refreshments to share if we found friends. We prayed that we would meet someone we knew and be able to get news from them about other Christian believers. We went back to our hotel and settled in the lobby to wait for the police.

Promptly at 10:30 p.m. two young "swingers" came to the lobby. They introduced themselves as the police from the CID, looked at our papers, and said, "Do not bring any letters in or out and do not disturb the orderly working of the camp. Is that okay?" "Yes," we said. They signed our papers. We went to bed thankful that the last hurdle seemed to have been crossed.

The next morning we took a taxi four miles out of town to a makeshift dock. We had been joined by a young Danish man named Hans Pieter who had shown up. He was working on "family reunification" with some Vietnamese who were already in Denmark. He was on official business. We adopted the same phrase to explain why we were going ... only it was family reunification for our church family—unofficial. The police had never checked with Hans; he just got phone permission. They never told him he couldn't carry letters out, which turned out to be a great blessing. In the camp we were asked to bring out literally hundreds of letters, but we told the people we had promised not to do it. Then we would point out that Hans Pieter did not have the same rule. On the return trip we found out he had a suitcase full of mail. And, since the people did not have access to postage, Hans said his organization would willingly apply the necessary stamps—another big blessing.

We waited and waited for the water tanker "Black Gold." It would take us three or more hours to get to Pulau Bidong.

It didn't come. At about 9:30 a.m. Ali (from the UN) showed up and told us we had to wait for 200 refugees who had just landed down the coast and would be joining us on the Black Gold, which had just arrived at our wharf. We got on board and waited some more, but no one showed up. About 10:30 a.m. the irritated and impatient captain said he was leaving, so Ali agreed the new refugees could come the next day, and we weighed anchor. The captain gruffly informed us we would have to be back on the boat by 3:00 p.m. to arrive home safely, since the Terengganu River had dangerous shifts during tide change and the ship could be overturned while trying to "cross the bar."

Now Ali came to us all upset. He had five hours of work to do on the island and he had decided to stay all night; he could not possibly get his work done between our late arrival and early departure. He asked us if we could get our work done in two hours? "No," we said, "that would be impossible. We should also stay all night." He agreed. Betty and I rejoiced at this new development; even though we had brought no extra clothes or toiletries. We had absolutely no idea who or what we would find on the island but a long visit was surely better than a short one, or so we figured.

An official contingent led by the Vietnamese camp commander and a lot of his staff met the boat. They expected 200 refugees on board which would have taken all their time and attention; instead, they had three people to welcome, so welcome us they did. We saw again how this entire trip had been orchestrated to our benefit, down to every detail. The camp commander, a former thoracic surgeon from Saigon, became our personal escort. After a sign-in procedure and a Malay police check (where we flashed our permits), we went to a briefing room to get the facts of the island and copies of figures and details. Hans was sent to a separate office to do his work, so Betty and I became the celebrities of the day.

We learned that six months earlier there was a huge exodus of boat people from Vietnam and there were 45,000 on the island at its peak. Now the camp held "only" 16,000 people and was "manageable." They had begun to do "forward planning." Many, many refugees followed us around and as we began to speak in Vietnamese the camp commander got very excited. When he learned that Betty had been a POW for eight months, he could not believe it. God gave us that key to an instant connection. He went everywhere for two days telling everybody, "*Hai ba hieu het*," meaning "these two women understand it all." He had been in "re-education" himself—a euphemism for a POW camp.

He took us on a tour of the camp in his vehicle. The organization of the camp which they divided into seven zones was very impressive. Each zone had a leader, committee, and school. We went to the refugee hospital they had made themselves; twenty-eight doctors served there. Six months earlier, at the height of the population surge there had been over 100 doctors. They had everything there including X-Ray equipment, an operating room and a pharmacy, even though the building itself was plywood and somewhat primitive.

After the hospital tour, we saw markets, a bakery (with an oven made out of a huge boulder), a hairdresser, and dwellings. Then, knowing we had been "religious workers" in Vietnam, he invited us to go to "religious hill"—an elevated place with three churches; Buddhist, Catholic, and Protestant (Tin Lanh). Each one had a courtyard, an office, and a place of worship. The Protestant, or Tin Lanh, section had a reading room made from an abandoned escape boat, which also served as the office.

Our "entourage" went into the Tin Lanh office and saw a young man reading the Bible. We told him we were looking for the pastor or head elder. Totally stunned, he ran off. Within a few minutes a young man came who was leader of the youth. He formally invited us to sit in the reading room which had lots of books and Christian literature—and you felt a bit like you were sitting in a boat looking out. Then they sent to find another person. Boiling hot tea showed up from somewhere which matched the stifling weather, but it was at least a liquid, as well as proper etiquette for us and the camp commander.

Just then, another person came running up the hill. I could not believe it and cried out in joy. It was a young man named Ho Xuan Phu—a friend of ours from Tam Ky in Quang Tin province. His father was a pastor and we had stayed nights in his home. His mother had severe arthritis and we had gotten special cortisone drugs for her. This was definitely the answer to our prayer to find someone we knew, because we knew him well. He had become one of the Tin Lanh leaders in the camp.

He told us his entire story, and then he said he had just sent a letter out to Grady Mangham with a list of names for resettlement through World Relief Commission. Thank goodness, in front of the camp commander Phu "legitimized" us and we realized he had done all our work as he gave us copies of his lists. These included the names of all Christians currently in the camp, and their home church of origin. Now, we were free to stay and enjoy the visit. Phu asked the commander for permission to hold a meeting that evening in the Tin Lanh Church, and he readily granted the request. Betty was to be the speaker and I would interpret into Vietnamese. Betty's Vietnamese was rusty; she fluently spoke the Raday language of the ethnic minority with whom she had worked. From the church we went to the dwelling of a Christian family and enjoyed a great meal. Each family in the camp was given one tin of baked beans, one tin of curried chicken, and one tin of sardines daily. They were also supplied with rice and oil. Some greens were grown locally and available in markets. The wonderful meal made us forget the meager circumstances of our surroundings as these displaced refugees hosted us in the most gracious manner.

As meeting time approached and we had not been free from the crowds following us all day we felt the need to use a "bathroom" or whatever passed for such. Finally, I asked to be shown the way, so most of the crowd followed us and waited outside the flimsy screen to be sure we made it. After that, they led us to the "guest hostel" where we would spend the night. It was a plywood building with a tin roof, high cutout windows and about 20 cots. The three of us and the boat captain were the only lodgers that night, unless you considered the mice we saw scurrying about. As I sat on the edge of my cot I got out a comb to do my hair, still windblown from the boat trip. Some young girls grabbed the comb and worked on me until they considered me presentable. They then escorted us in a procession back to Religious Hill to have our evening service.

The little plywood building was full to the walls; every bench had improbable numbers of people on it and there were people sitting in the windows and crowded all outside. The camp commander came and sat on the front row. Someone had gotten the word out! Someone else had rigged up a makeshift PA system. Betty and I wedged through the crowd to the front where we had two seats reserved for us. Considering the short notice and the circumstances, the program was absolutely remarkable: lots of singing, special music, and impromptu poems and reading of Scripture. After a long time, Betty gave her testimony and I translated. The dear people there really related to Betty. And when she quoted the famous slogan of "Uncle Ho" (Ho Chi Minh, the revolutionary hero and leader), the house went wild. Yes, he said, *"Khong co gi quy hon doc lap tu gio"* meaning, "Nothing is more precious than Freedom and Independence!" We finally got escorted by loads of people down to our "guest house" accommodations and fell asleep fully dressed on the cots, wrapped cozily in our mosquito nets.

The next morning, by previous agreement, the camp commander came early to take us from zone to zone where we had a brief English lesson in each of the schools. It was a joy to see how these adults, youth, and children eagerly tried to prepare themselves for what would come next in their lives. We had a lot of laughter and joy as we taught for thirty short minutes in each makeshift school. Again, a Christian family hosted us for a "Central Vietnam menu" lunch and we had prayer together with our new "brothers and sisters" on Pulau Bidong.

The 200 new refugees came on the Black Gold boat that noon; huddled, seasick, bewildered, and frightened. We saw how the camp sprang into action to care for them and get them assimilated with the others, and we were happy that the worst part of their journey to freedom was over. We three got back on the Black Gold and sat together processing our twenty-four hours with the refugees. We had lots of messages to pass on, and lots of memories of resilience and strength. We landed in Terengganu, had a good night's sleep in our hotel, and headed home by plane to our own island, Penang, the next day.

By the time Bidong was closed in 1991, about 250,000 refugees went through the camp before being accepted mostly by the United States, Canada, Australia, and France. After the camp was closed, many refugees were deported back to Vietnam. The forced repatriation met strong protests from the remaining refugees. This island was only one of many refuges for the "boat people"; Indonesia, Hong Kong, Thailand, and the Philippines also received them. But Pulau Bidong was the largest.

In 1996, Sungei Besi, the transit camp, closed. Later, Over 9,000 Vietnamese refugees were repatriated back to Vietnam. On August 28, 2005 the last Vietnamese refugees were repatriated, and the period of the boat people, which some called the "liquid Auschwitz," was over. And Phu . . . Phu became the leader of a Vietnamese Christian publishing organization in California and raised his family there. Neither of us will forget the "shock and awe" of seeing each other again on Religious Hill on Pulau Bidong.

[1] Excerpts of information taken from Wikipedia, the free encyclopedia

CHAPTER 27

THE TRIAL

W e arrived at our sixth and final year at Dalat School. Along with his regular work, Woody had completed his master's degree in Christian Ministry at Singapore Bible College and was now director of Dalat. We were sponsors for the senior class of 1980, and preparing for home assignment at the end of the semester. I taught Bible, directed the school play, and played general hostess for Dalat. Life was busy, full, and rewarding.

And then one day in early March I got a totally unexpected call from the American Embassy in Kuala Lumpur (K.L.), the capital of Malaysia. The caller told me they desperately needed my help in a UN trial currently in progress as an interpreter for the Vietnamese victim of an alleged rape. I was stunned. "Where did they get my name?" I asked. "I have only spoken Vietnamese about five days in the last six years," I sputtered. "I have a job here that I cannot leave," I maintained. "Furthermore, I have never learned rape vocabulary," was my final clincher. All this time he had remained silent.

Then he responded, "It would only be for a few days and we will pay all your expenses. Furthermore, we cannot find anyone else that can understand and speak both Vietnamese and English." Well, I have always said that "three little words will take me almost anywhere." Those three little words are "all expenses paid!" I began to imagine the Vietnamese woman aligned against a court system and I realized I could probably arrange to be away for a few days. These thoughts, coupled with my sense of adventure and love of a new story, caused me to say, "Yes." Above all, there was the compelling thought that this might somehow be a "God-thing" in my life.

By the next day I had bought airline tickets, arranged for my classes to be covered, signed Woody up in the dining room for meals, and packed my suitcase. That evening I boarded the plane for the forty-five minute flight to K.L. where I was taken to a hotel in the city of Klang, about 45 minutes away. There they told me the details of the trial.

A Vietnamese refugee, with her family, was one of hundreds in the transit center called Sungei Besi. Her family had been accepted into the United States and were getting final health checks and paperwork completed. While undergoing lab tests she alleged that she was raped by an Indian man who was a Malaysian citizen. Before this, she and her husband had been asked to perform sexual acts in his presence so that he could collect "specimens." Then he told the husband to leave and told her he had to test her and then raped her. She and her husband were so upset by this that they reported this to the Malaysians, and asked if this was truly required? They made a deposition to the Malaysian police in Vietnamese, which was translated to Malay.

The Malaysians reported this to the UNHCR. The UN authorities, suspecting that this may be happening on a regular basis, decided to bring the man to trial. The accused hired a very well-known Indian lawyer and now the case had been called to trial. It was a high profile case supervised totally by the UN and reported in all the papers. This is where I came in.

Since Sungei Besi camp was technically outside the K.L. city limits, the trial was held in Klang, the royal capital of the State of Selangor about twenty miles west of K.L. Port Klang is among the top twenty container ports in the world, is a modern city and the residence of the Sultan of Selangor.

The next morning a driver took me to the Klang courthouse, and I entered a courtroom for the first time in my life. The scene was bedlam. The gallery was full of observers from the media and the UN. One section was reserved for about twenty Vietnamese who were being detained for the duration of the trial since they might have information. Since the court followed the British system of a "magistrate's trial," there was no jury but the judge sat on an elevated platform behind a kind of desk. The two lawyers and their clients were in the front row on opposite sides of an aisle. Court reporters, interns, translators, and various functionaries were seated in a row across the front. There was a stage with an elevated witness stand surrounded by chest-high walls . . . a sort of "box," which looked like a pulpit to me. Each witness would go up the steps to this position to give his/her testimony.

To add to the confusion, a drama in progress outside the window occupied everyone's attention: a monkey had snatched two kittens from a mother cat and had swung up into a high branch holding them. The cat tried hard to get her babies back and the courtroom crowd cheered for one side or the other. Then the bailiff called the crowd to order as the Judge entered and took his place; the Honorable Mohammed Ali.

The first item of business was to call me to the stand to take two oaths: the interpreter's oath, and my personal oath. Then the defense attorney, or lawyer for the accused man, questioned me extensively about my ability. I answered, apparently satisfactorily because I was "seated" on a high stool next to the witness box. Then the woman, the alleged victim, was called to the stand. She had a court appointed "plaintiff's attorney" who had no way to communicate directly with her. She came slowly forward, staring at me with hopeless eyes, looking sixty years old. She was thirty-nine. She got into the box and the bailiff began to swear her in. As I interpreted his words to her, a transformation came over her face. She began to talk rapidly to me about the fact I was able to speak Vietnamese to her. She took the oath and I think she had her first glimmer of hope.

Unbelievably, she had a *Hue* accent, distinctive to that city and quite hard to understand. But we had had much contact with people, especially refugees, from that area so I was able to understand almost everything on the first try. They conducted the trial in English and followed the process of a British magistrate's trial. For some reason, no taped recordings were allowed, and the judge wrote all the answers down in longhand himself. I could see from the beginning this would take a LONG time. The questions were put in English, I translated into Vietnamese, the answers were given, I translated back into English, the judge wrote it all down, and things slowly proceeded from one background question to another. Twelve o'clock—lunchtime recess declared. The Vietnamese retreated to wherever they were taken, the judge invited me to lunch with him, and everyone dispersed.

The first three mornings proceeded in this manner. Each lunch the judge kindly took me to a local restaurant, along with a tableful of others from the courtroom. We could not, of course, talk about the trial but we had great conversation about life in Malaysia. My expenses were paid, but I was never sure who picked up the tab. By 2:30 p.m. we reassembled in the courtroom and the pace proceeded. Often, I had to rephrase the question two or three ways, either because of my poor translation, or her total inability to understand the reason for the question. She was a country woman from the vicinity of Hue, wanting only to get on her way to

California, but finding herself embroiled in a drama beyond her comprehension.

At 4:30 p.m. that first day was over and we had not even gotten near the substance of the trial. The judge instructed a court officer to take me to the "Government Rest House," the name of hostels operated by the government for public officials. These ranged from lovely hotels to primitive camps, so I had no idea what to expect. The one I went to was nice. It was built of wood, Malay style. I cannot even remember many details about it except that I was the only female in the establishment and there were a lot of men. I went to the dining room for supper where I had to sit at a bar surrounded by curious men. I ate a quiet meal. I went back to my room. There was no lock on the door and no screens in the window, so I crawled under the mosquito net and went to bed, if not to sleep, early. But my expenses there were paid.

The first thing next morning I called an American girlfriend of mine named Jacquetta, who lived in K.L. Her husband headed up an American company with factories based there. I had met her at Dalat when she came to play the piano for the musical groups from the International School in K.L. who had come for a competition. She stayed in our home and we made a great connection based on our common faith. She was beautiful, capable, musical, delightful, and ... she had a lovely home in K.L. that I had visited. I told her my plight and asked her if I could stay with her. She readily agreed and even offered to pick me up that afternoon and transport me back and forth. That made a huge difference in my outlook.

Friday afternoon near "closing time" the trial trudged on not even near the main part of the story, so the judge peremptorily said, "Court in recess until Tuesday morning at 10:00 a.m." What? I called the airport and got a ticket back to Penang. Jacquetta went home because the judge asked the defense lawyer to take me to the airport in his fancy sports convertible. I wish I could have recorded that most interesting conversation as we drove along. I flew home and rearranged my life, with apologies to all, for one more week. At Dalat, they really didn't have "subs" for the classes; a friend would take your class in an emergency or illness, but you ran out of friends fast if the emergency was going to last awhile.

Due to government holidays, there were only three days of trial the next week. We finally got into the substance of the accusation and it was nasty. I had read the "rape stories" in the Bible to try to get vocabulary; I had everyone at the school praying for me, but these counter accusations rang hollow and ridiculous. The woman and her family did not understand the "alternate theory" his lawyer was presenting. She just kept saying, "No, no, no." It was awful. Jacquetta came and stayed in the gallery every day. The judge included her in his invitations to lunch. He often talked "theoretically" about what constituted rape, and what we should do if we were ever raped, God forbid. (That would be scratch, bite or otherwise leave a mark on the perpetrator to prove it was forced, by the way.)

At one point the defense lawyer was going over the deposition made to the Malay police. It was given in Vietnamese through an English speaker who gave it to the police who recorded it in Malay. The lawyer would take one word, translate it into English, and then I would translate it into Vietnamese. He would ask her if she had used that word. Now it is out of context and passed through five translations. Of course she said no. When I would try to explain what she had said in the original, the lawyer would scream that I could only interpret words, not cultures. I wanted to stipulate that she did agree to the deposition as a whole, just not every word as he presented it. He called for impeachment of the witness. Now I was stuck. I wasn't sure what that meant, let alone how to interpret it. The judge settled it by overruling his motion.

Once again, by the end of the week, I could see the clock ticking. Before the Friday afternoon session, I asked to see the judge in his chambers. I told him that I had been told this would be over quickly, that I had a job to do, that we were getting ready to leave for our furlough, and that I would have to resign, with apologies. "Fine, Mrs. Stemple," he said. "You can resign, but we will hold your passport until the trial is over." Oops, I wasn't going anywhere. So that afternoon, I flew back to Dalat where I had become somewhat of a celebrity. Every day the history teacher at Dalat, under the guise of "Current Events" would read all the sordid events about the rape trial which made daily headlines. The paper often referred to or quoted the American interpreter which made the kids so happy!

Reluctantly, I returned to Klang for the third time to resume the trial. This time it got even worse. By the second morning questions were being asked which were intensely personal, and so the judge would call "in camera," meaning all observers had to go out. Then I would translate for the woman, she would answer, and I would translate back to the judge. Everyone would come back in; a few questions later, the scene would be repeated. Everyone got to hear the question, but no one except the officials got to hear the answer. It was like a circus; the concepts they explored were very hard to translate. Even I could not have answered the questions they asked her.

At one point, after a very difficult question when everyone was out of the room, the woman began beating her head and shouting "*ngu, ngu, ngu.*" While I was hitting my head and translating, "I'm so stupid, I'm so stupid," she suddenly slumped in the box, unconscious. I was able to catch her as she fell and to hold her while the judge called to bring in her husband, at which point all the spectators came running into the courtroom. Some Vietnamese helped to stretch her out on the front bench and they began vigorously trying to revive her.

The strong aroma of Tiger Balm began to fill the air. This is the all-purpose Vietnamese salve which is a remedy for any ailment. If you have a headache, you pinch it between your eyes; for a stomach ache or nausea, rub it on your abdomen; for aching joints, massage it into the affected part. I am a firm believer and user of Tiger Balm; it is a combination of menthol, eucalyptus, and other mysterious ingredients and it works. For fainting, first you put some just under the nose; if this stimulation is not effective, you take a coin such as a quarter and use the coin to score the Tiger Balm across the kidney areas. As someone did this she began to stir, but was very groggy. After about five minutes when the ministrations were not effective, the judge said, "Take her to the hospital. Everyone else is in recess until this afternoon." He proceeded to invite Jacquetta and me out to lunch.

I could not think of eating. I asked the judge for permission to visit the victim in the local hospital, which he granted. Jacquetta willingly drove her beautiful Mercedes down to the crowded streets where the public welfare hospital was and we went in to inquire where our Vietnamese friend was located. As we found the ward full of beds our eyes went immediately to a bed in the center with a policeman standing at the foot. As we neared the bed this poor Vietnamese woman looked at us and began to sob with relief. She had awakened to find herself in a hospital ward full of Malay women and no one who could speak her language. She was tied hand and foot with soft restraints and had no idea how she had gotten there. I was very angry.

I said to the policeman, "Untie her." "But she is a prisoner," he said. "Look at her," I replied, "she is so weak she could not get out of the bed. Furthermore, she is NOT a prisoner. Untie her." So he did. "Now," I ordered, "you go stand by the door. You can see her perfectly well from there—this women's ward is no place for a man to be." He willingly went to the door. Then I turned to one of the nurses and said, "Give her a drink." She rushed to do it. Jacquetta was watching round-eyed. I bent to the lady and told her, "We are going to the market to get you some things for your care. We will be back in thirty minutes." She soberly watched us go, as though her lifeline was being taken away.

I asked Jacquetta if she had some Malaysian money for the market, because I did not have much. She did. She expertly navigated that big car right down to the middle of the market. We went in and got everything I had ever seen brought in to care for a patient; towels and a basin, a thermos for hot water, a teapot and cups, oranges, peanuts, sweetened condensed milk, toothbrush and paste, a little mirror, a comb and a sweater. We got it all piece by piece and carried it to the car. Back to the hospital and into the ward, laden with the items, we went. As she saw us come in the door, she rose up in her bed in absolute relief and a happy smile lit her face. We had returned. Jacquetta, overcome with emotion at the woman's response, dropped her items on the stand and spread herself out over the victim—cheek to cheek, chest to chest, arms to arms—and began to sob. I saw something in that moment of the real meaning of compassion; not pity, but love and empathy mixed in a full expression of the heart of Christ. The scene is forever framed in my mind; and it was priceless.

We went back to the courtroom to hear the judge say, "Trial is in recess until this woman can testify. Come back in two weeks." I was able to call the UN representative and ask, well actually demand, that a person who spoke Vietnamese and English be sent to stay with the woman until she was released. Their mandate, after all, was to help the helpless and once they were aware of the situation, they more than cared for the woman. Jacquetta took me to the airport and I flew back to Penang, unexpectedly soon.

On the appointed day, I again appeared at the courtroom. As I perched on my stool by the witness box, they called for the woman to come in. Again, the room was packed. She very slowly made her way from the door, down the aisle, to the front. She looked even older and very, very tired. She stared blankly up at the judge, and he immediately said, "She is in no condition to stand trial. Case is in recess for one more week." I could not get a plane that day, so I bought tickets on a local train that seemed to stop at every tin mine along the route, not to mention the towns and villages. I was in despair that this trial would ever end. I had called Woody and asked him to meet me at Butterworth train station on the mainland, but with every clack of the train wheels I was asking myself, "What am I going to do to get out of this?"

As we went back across the ferry to Penang Island and drove to our home, Woody gave me a thick pack of notes and letters. They were from the high school students who thought I would be spending the week in Klang and had asked Woody to send the messages to me. When I got to my room and spread them out to read them, I was amazed. What wisdom and cheer and encouragement those students had sent me. They also reminded me of things I had known all along: how God knew where I was and had a purpose in it; how God was using me there with the Vietnamese at the trial; how I was possibly the only person in Malaysia who could do this; and lots of little jokes and comments that brought me back to reality. I prayed and thanked God for His reminders through these great kids, and I quit trying to figure out how to do things my way, or "get out of" something special God had for me.

But I still was not a very happy interpreter as I made my fifth trip to K.L. and on to the Klang courtroom. I greeted the woman's lawyer out in the hall, and then went in to take my usual high, uncomfortable, backless stool. As soon as the judge took his bench and called the court into session, the defense lawyer jumped to his feet. "Your honor," he said loudly, "I demand a retrial." Then he went on to say "Look at Mrs. Stemple here. She is the only person in the room who has understood both languages. Up to now, I have trusted her totally. But just this morning, I saw her speaking outside the courtroom with the woman's lawyer. I believe she is working with him and therefore a biased interpreter. I cannot trust her." I was in shock and everyone was staring at me. The woman's lawyer jumped up to explain that we only said hello, and that we were in a public entryway with many people around us. A shouting match erupted until the judge banged his gavel and called for a recess. He went to his chambers.

Everyone sat in silence staring at me and the Vietnamese had no clue what was happening. By now, I had formed a conclusion that the accused lab technician had, in fact, done what they said he had done. The husband and wife were sorry for reporting it because now they, and all who were with them in the transit center, had to stay until the trial was over. If they had kept quiet they would have been in the United States long ago. Now it seemed we were at an impasse. Then a bailiff told me the judge wanted to see me in chambers.

"Mrs. Stemple," Judge Mohammed Ali told me, "you have done a wonderful job. You have done nothing wrong. But this lawyer for the accused is very clever and he will use every legal opportunity to derail or stall this trial. Therefore, I have no choice but to let you go, and resume when we find a new interpreter. We will go back into the courtroom and remain silent for five minutes while you explain to the Vietnamese in their language what is happening." "Thank you, judge," I said. And, under my breath, "and thank you, God, this is what I have been praying for."

After a good talk with all the assembled Vietnamese, and with my arm around the woman, I explained that I had been fired. Then, I said a lot more which shall remain between us about their situation and their hopes and dreams of a better life when they got to America. I called Woody and giddily told him I'd be home that night. The next day the headlines in large type read, "AMERICAN INTERPRETER FIRED FROM RAPE TRIAL FOR BIAS." The article, although factual, did not begin to describe the emotions of that day. In the end, the embarrassment was well worth the cost as I had been miraculously extracted from that trial.

A few weeks later we went home as scheduled on our furlough. I had made five trips to Kuala Lumpur, spent eleven days in the Klang courtroom, and had an experience I would never want to repeat. But a dear Vietnamese woman was in the courtroom over seven months before the trial, which began on March 5, finally came to an end in mid-October. And the accused man was found innocent. The family was resettled in California. I asked to have information to contact them, but privacy laws forbid them giving me any information. They did tell me she had a child; the timing suggested it was conceived in the Sungei Besi transit center.

CELEBRATION

Our lives seemed far removed from Vietnam when Woody became pastor of a church in Jamestown, New York. We settled in to American life and only had sporadic news from Vietnam. Each Christmas we sent a fair amount of money through "sources" to friends in Danang: a pastor's widow, our former workers, and a pastor's wife who disbursed it as requested for special needs. Then we moved to Rome, New York and learned of the extensive refugee resettlement program in nearby Utica. For several years I was able to teach English and American culture, as well as "troubleshoot" family problems with the Vietnamese community there. It was a special joy for me to work with the large influx of Amerasians that were allowed to come to the United States. These were now young adults and hopeful for acceptance in American culture that they had never achieved in their home country.

We really longed to return and visit Vietnam and wondered if it would ever be possible. We resolved not to go unless it would be safe for the people we visited. A few of our former colleagues had gone back, but their movements were carefully monitored and any meetings with believers had to be conducted clandestinely. Meanwhile, our son Stewart prepared academically to return to Asia in business. He took immersion Chinese for one year at Cornell University and could read, write, and speak the language. Armed with an MBA in International Business, he moved to Hong Kong in 1991 and became very conversant with the Asian scene.

In 1992 he visited Vietnam and told us it was safe to return. In January 1993 we joined him in Ho Chi Minh City (HCMC), formerly known to us as Saigon. He had prepared for our trip by reporting each stop with the government and using a government approved car and driver. We were able to drive on Route One all the way from Saigon to Danang, something we had never done before due to war conditions. At first, we were careful about what we said even though our driver said he did not know English. But as we got close to Quang Ngai province, we could not contain ourselves. We told the driver to stop at every Tin Lanh Church—and he did.

It had been 25 years since we had lived in central Vietnam. Since the people there had not been permitted to move, we knew who we would find at each place—if they were still alive. As we would turn off the road into the courtyard or driveway of the church, people would hesitantly come out of the parsonage to check us out. When they recognized us, they would shout, grab our hands and pull us into their homes for tea. Often, they would jokingly call, *"Con Ma, Con Ma!"* (these are ghosts). They could not believe we were suddenly walking into their lives after all these years. We would all be talking at once trying to catch up on the time apart. They could not believe that "little Stewart," a Quang Ngai son, was now a young man. Although they were very cautious about discussing their situations they exuberantly praised God for reuniting us. Over and over they said, "We did not think we would see you again until heaven."

We spent the night in a government hotel north of the river in Quang Ngai; it had not been built when we were there. It was quite comical in a way because I think we were the only guests in the hotel, which was a "Russian-looking" utilitarian cement building. There was no dining room open, and no taxi or cyclo to take us into town which was about a mile away. So the three Stemples walked into town with half the hotel staff following us to see where we were going. We went to a restaurant and sent word that we were in town ... before long we met up with many of our friends, who caught us up on their news.

The next day we learned that our former church in town had been destroyed when the new government took over. However the one built outside of town, that was strong as a fortress, was still meeting regularly and the people there had remained just as strong. We went to see our former house and neighborhood; the house was gone and we could not even figure out many neighborhood landmarks. It was a bitter-sweet visit for us, but we were so glad we were able to go.

We drove on up to Danang and continued to stop at all the Tin Lanh churches receiving the same wonderful reception along the way. By now, our driver was looking forward to his many "tea parties." Someone had gone ahead and told the Danang pastor and wife that we were coming because they were waiting when we arrived. Faithful and true, they stood in the doorway of their home to share tea with us and tell us about the family of God and how they had fared. People in the neighborhood, including "Sister Ten" and her family, all came by. That night, even though it was not really permitted, they hosted a wonderful dinner for us in a back Sunday School room. All the Danang pastors and wives were there sharing their stories of the hard years. Tears of joy and tears of sorrow, but mostly tears of love, flowed freely—and there was much gratitude that the church was so strong.

We stayed downtown in a hotel by the river and I could not sleep that night; the stories we had heard and the loyalty and love of our friends overwhelmed me. The next day, Co Thoi came to visit and took us for *pho*, the wonderful "signature Vietnamese" noodle soup and we flew back to Ho Chi Minh City and home. I have been back seven other times, usually leading groups, but none of those trips begins to match the poignancy of that first trip. Each time I go, I see much more development, more outward freedoms, and a stronger and larger Tin Lanh church.

In 1994 after the United States lifted the trade embargo with Vietnam, it became like the "wild west" for business expansion. All contracts had to be initiated, certified, and permitted in Hanoi, the capital, but the "boom" flourished all over the country. Our son Stewart was hired by U.S. private investors to establish a joint venture investment with the Vietnam tourist bureau. He set up an office in Hanoi in the downstairs of a modern house with his lodging upstairs. This was in the lovely old section of the city and right next door to the Vice President, Madame Binh, with whom he became good friends. Stewart was very well received there since he spoke the language which came back to him from his childhood. The photo section of the Vietnamese Sunday newspaper had a two-page spread about him with a photo of him windsurfing on West Lake. It praised his love for the Vietnamese people and said he was 'the son of religious teachers who were in Vietnam before the revolution." No secrets.

I was able to go visit him in Hanoi, which I had never been able to visit before. It is a beautiful city, and the people were welcoming and friendly. Even during that first visit they had mostly "forgotten" the war, and by now it remains long in the past. They said, "We had 1000 years with the Chinese, and eventually we defeated them; we had 100 years with the French, and eventually defeated them; we had ten years with the Americans, and now they are gone. We are like bamboo—we bend clear over, but we snap back up." It seems true; they are resilient, and they bear no long-lasting animosity toward America or Americans; in fact, they love to have us there.

I worked hard to hear and respond to the distinctive northern accent. I loved going to worship at the historic Tin Lanh church which had remained open all during the conflict. Stewart was able to start an International Church in his home, along with other expatriates, beginning with eight people. Today, that same church meets in a hotel, but now has over 300 in regular attendance. As from the beginning, only holders of foreign passports are permitted to attend.

Those of us, Americans and Canadians who had served in the missionary family in Vietnam, formed a strong bond. One of us, Marge Cline, has agreed to keep an address list of us all. When anyone writes a newsletter, or has a prayer need, or wants to share information, we send it to Marge. She sends it to the list. When political developments occur, or a colleague passes away, or something newsworthy takes place from any of us, we all hear about it. No week passes without at least one communication from Marge, and often quite a few. Thank you, Marge—and Normadine and Lil, your subs when you go away. We never want to lose what we gained in those intense days in Vietnam.

No matter where we have gone in our post-Vietnam days, we continue to be blessed with connections with Vietnamese. When Woody and I moved to Cleveland I became acquainted with a dear widow named Mrs. Huu Ba Le when I was asked to help her plan a Christian funeral for her husband. This developed into a wonderful friendship as I weekly went to her home for over a year to help teach her in her newfound faith. It is still a good day when we meet or telephone to catch up on news.

And I must mention the wonderful story of Pastor Cang Dang who escaped Vietnam by boat with his wife and 12 children, the youngest of whom was 2 weeks old. He is still pastoring a Vietnamese congregation at The Chapel in Akron, Ohio; the church which sponsored them over thirty years ago. We go there when we can on holidays — not only for the wonderful choirs and program, but also because Mrs. Dang supervises an unbelievable buffet of food, most of which she has prepared herself. And, we recently enjoyed attending the wedding of that baby boy refugee who is now a doctor. All twelve children are highly educated, most with doctorates. Each in his or her own way is contributing greatly to U.S. society, as well as serving in the church. The oldest, Pastor Minh Dang, is taking over for his father as lead pastor, and also effectively helping the church in Vietnam with training and support. He has helped me so much with contacts and information for each visit I take back. Visiting in their home is a high honor for us and overwhelms us with memories.

The year 2005 marked the thirtieth anniversary of the "Fall of Saigon" which effectively ended the war. The Vietnamese District of The C&MA in the United States, headquartered in Anaheim CA, planned a wonderful celebration at Azusa Pacific University to celebrate the growth of the Church "in diaspora." They invited all former Vietnam missionaries to attend the four-day event and covered everyone's airfare, housing and meal expenses. Woody and I joined about forty of our colleagues to hear and see (and taste!) the wonderful things God has done in the church. The music, much of it contemporary and composed by the Vietnamese, was wonderful. We met many old friends that we did not even realize had emigrated to the U.S. and got caught up on so much that had happened in those thirty years. All the missionaries were honored at a very special ceremony and given gifts and flowers. Tears of joy were flowing freely.

Saturday of the conference was divided into Men's Day and Women's Day. I was honored to be invited to give the talk at the Women's Day of the celebration. The topic was "How to Pass Your Faith on to the Next Generation." It was a BIG "stretch" as I was asked to give the message in Vietnamese. How wonderful to have son Stewart join me and give his side of the topic, also in Vietnamese. When I introduced him and said he was still single, he brought down the house with his quotation from "Uncle Ho," "Nothing is More Precious than Freedom and Independence!"

Today, according to estimated figures from Vietnam, there are over 200,000 believers in North Vietnam and about 1,500,000 followers of Christ in South Vietnam. What a wonderful tribute to God's faithfulness and to the testimony of growth under repression. This is an encouragement and joy to all of us who served there.

Yes, we still try to get Vietnamese food whenever we can, and have found the best places for *cha gios* (fried spring rolls) and *pho* (the signature noodle soup). Our great desire is to complete our stories and dedicate them to the wonderful church in Vietnam on the occasion of their one hundredth anniversary in June 2011 in our hometown of Danang. Our whole family is hoping to make the trip to celebrate together. We will carry back the certificate showing Woody as an honorary citizen of Danang and see if it makes a difference! It does to us.

CHAPTER 28

we visit leaders

Back with my girlfriends!

Pastor Châu

ACKNOWLEDGEMENTS

Writing this book has been a journey of learning for me. So many contributed to the work that it would be impossible to name them all. My husband, Woody, has been my anchor, my helper, my proofreader, my financier, my soother, my example, and my reality check. I would never have started, let alone completed the project without his love and steady presence.

Our elder son Stewart, who lives in Hong Kong, could write his own book since he inherited the "chance-of-a-lifetime" love of travel and daily drama from me. He has been in the Asian business world since 1991 with great effectiveness in training leaders. At the invitation of the Chinese government, he carried the Olympic torch in Xiamen Province in 2008. Stewart is a great communicator. We are so proud of his life and many accomplishments, but our love for him is because of who he is! Thank you for using well the many gifts God has given you, and for your strong and faithful love for us and for God. And thank you for being part of this project—in life and in encouragement.

Our younger son Sam, with his beautiful wife Jen, lives in Germany with our four perfect grandchildren, Jordan, Ellie, Matthew, and Katie. Sam is the Chaplain at Black Forest Academy, an international boarding school originally for the children of missionaries. I can't wait for them to read the story together, especially the chapters of life as their Dad knew it as a boy. Leaving them this book as a legacy was one of the foundational reasons for writing it. Thank you for being exactly who you are and I love you all dearly. I am so proud to be your Oma.

Since this is not an autobiography, I have written nothing about our lives prior to our marriage. Thank you to our parents (now deceased) and brothers and sisters and their families for their contribution to who we are. These past years have brought special joy and encouragement as we have shared times with Gail and John and Mary and Phil.

Thank you to the Shell Point Community, especially the Village Church and Pastor Ken who gave me a secret room in which to work. Peter Dys, administrator, was an early encourager. Others like Dottie Morrison and Bonnie Palmquist gave me the needed push to begin. Hallie Cirino, creative writing teacher at Shell Point, did some early editing and gave me helpful hints.

My summer Beulah Beach community, led by Ralph and Kathy Trainer, has also been encouraging, letting me run in and out of their office for help. Crystal Missler, the awesome comm team leader here, gave invaluable advice and help on the graphics. This place is my "soul home" and I felt best completing the project here. Gail Krauss, my neighbor and prayer partner in both summer and winter locations, pops in often to share words of wisdom, focused prayer, and sometimes banana bread.

Thank you to my Vietnamese friends, such as Pastor Minh Dang in Akron, Tuyet Collacott in Vancouver, Henry Fahman in southern California, and Gwen Khang Nguyen in San Jose. Each of them has incredibly busy lives, but took time to help me with Vietnamese sensitivities, spelling, and other helpful advice.

Thank you to proofreaders like Twila Petrie in England, who warned me she would be meticulous, and who ended up using almost all the advice in the *The Chicago Manual of Style* to get me straightened out. If there are any errors, I guarantee they are not her fault! Lois Olmstead in Montana is my successful author and columnist friend who encouraged me to get going and gave lots of good advice about the whole adventure of self-publishing.

A huge thankful shout out to Mark Sasse, my pro bono Editor, who is an English teacher and wonderful friend. He made me get out of passive voice and into active in every chapter. Most of my pages had more red ink than typing when he got done with me! And as soon as I saw it, I knew he was right. He and his family spent several years teaching English in Vietnam, so he knows the cultural nuances well. In fact, while there, he wrote monthly monographs on different cultural ideas which should have been published as a book. Thanks to Mark's wife, Karen, who let him spend half his vacation time on my project. I owe Mark a debt of gratitude I could never fully pay. Thank you.

I have to mention "Sandusky Sandy" who brought us meals so I could work without interruption, and John and Barb Sutherland who had "game night" with us twice a week to relax my brain.

And, thanks to all my "Sunday letter" recipients ... and many other friends ... who have prayed for me through this project. You know who you are, including Marge, Sally, and Nancy. Prayer has not been "the least you could do" ... really, it is the most you can do! Thanks for all the title suggestions and words of wisdom. Don't stop praying now! Pray for a wide reception.

I know I am leaving out a host of people who contributed to my life and to the writing of this book; and I ask your forgiveness. If we go to reprint, I will include you.

Most of all, I give thanks to God, who birthed the project in my heart, gave me creativity and energy to complete it, and now has my full cooperation to take it wherever He wants it to go.

CPSIA information can be obtained at www.ICGtesting.com
Printed in the USA
BVOW080843300812

299161BV00002B/2/P